MW00490873

Praise for *Hummingbird: Messages from My Ancestors*

"Diana Raab's *Hummingbird* is far more than a memoir. It is a creative collage that offers hope, guidance, and inspiration for those willing to follow her on an inner journey to the wisdom of experience and ancestral trauma with an added touch of guidance for anyone looking to process their own life's transformations."

~ Matthew J. Pallamary, author of *Spirit Matters* and *Picaflor*

"Like the tiny bird with the amazing heart who is her spirit guide, Diana Raab encourages us in *Hummingbird* to stop, wait, watch, and remember, mining the wisdom of the past, looking to the future, yet all the while enjoying the sweetness life has to offer in the current moment."

~ Darlyn Finch Kuhn, author of *Red Wax Rose*, *Three Houses*, and *Sewing Holes*

"What a beautiful memoir, with so many revelations of the healing journey, and I love the prompts in each chapter. This book takes you on a journey and then gives you an opportunity to do your own self-reflection. Beautiful work!"

~ Christine Corrigan Mendez, EdM, LPC NCC

"In tender and graceful prose, Diana Raab's memoir *Hummingbird* examines the experiences that have shaped her, however painful they may be. Her personal stories of hope and loss, illness and joy, and love and neglect invite us to reflect on our own ancestral influences and their role in shaping who we are today. Iridescent, *Hummingbird* dips, dives, and hovers. A beautiful, rewarding read."

~ Cati Porter, author of *small mammals*

"Raab points out we receive many messages if we are aware of and in tune with our feelings and thoughts. If she can do this, obviously others are able to as well. The hummingbird is a recurring "character" who brings joy, guidance, and direction to her life. Clues to receiving messages are included for those who may wish to follow a similar path. This book imparts wisdom and encouragement for responding to our inner voices. It is almost a guidebook to help us live life to the fullest. Memorable episodes will have the readers thinking about the book in the future and seeing life with a new perspective. Refreshing and hopeful!"

~ Carolyn Wilhelm, *Midwest Book Review*

"In her eloquent and soul-searching *Hummingbird*, Diana Raab holds a mirror up to her own life, chronicling pain and renewal, while offering readers a way in, creatively, to take stock of their own. With its sweeping subtitle, *Messages from My Ancestors*, this book is both a heartfelt memoir of several generations and a catalyst for the spiritual practice of writing as a way of healing."

~ Roy Hoffman, author of
The Promise of the Pelican

"*Hummingbird* offers us sage advice on how to work through challenging times. Raab stresses the importance of journaling and its capacity to help us keep our heads above water while we navigate life. At the end of each chapter, she provides powerful writing prompts that allow us to go deep to access our own stories. She also offers words of wisdom we should all live by. Speaking of her grandmother, Raab says, 'She taught me the importance of living each day to its fullest and as if it were my last.' This is an insightful and important book about love, surrender, and acceptance."

~ Maureen Phillips, teacher, writer, editor

"In *Hummingbird*, Raab focuses on how examining the lives of those who've most influenced us can offer perspective, assist us through challenges, reinforce gratitude, bring joy and comfort, and help us live life more fully. Through telling stories and offering writing prompts, Raab provides a valuable roadmap for understanding our own lives by connecting to the past."

~ Nancy McCabe, author of *Vaulting through Time* and *Can This Marriage Be Saved? A Memoir*

"Diana Raab is always at her best when she inspires her readers with the up close and spiritual. Her new memoir, *Hummingbird*, does exactly that, and her writing prompts make it a practical must read for any author in need of a creative nudge. The memories of storytelling ancestors are sure to be a bonus that will soon leave this book dog eared from the rereading of it."

~ Carolyn Howard-Johnson, author of *Imperfect Echoes*, a *Writers Digest*-honored book of poetry

"This is a lovely book: uplifting and inspiring, full of wisdom and unconditional love, even for those who have hurt the author. She reveals herself, perhaps unknowingly, as a mature spirit, and her words will help you to follow her. At one level, the book is instructive in how to use journaling for self-healing, but it is much more. It is also indirectly instructive in how to heal physically, mentally, and spiritually. Highly recommended."

~ Bob Rich, PhD, author of *From Depression to Contentment*

HUMMINGBIRD

Dedicated to my children, grandchildren,
and future great grandchildren

HUMMINGBIRD

MESSAGES FROM
MY ANCESTORS

A Memoir with
Reflection and Writing Prompts

Diana Raab

Modern History Press
Ann Arbor, MI

ISBN 978-1-61599-764-0 paperback
ISBN 978-1-61599-765-7 hardcover
ISBN 978-1-61599-766-4 eBook

Modern History Press   www.LHPress.com
5145 Pontiac Trail   info@LHPress.com
Ann Arbor, MI 48105   Tollfree 888-761-6268

Distributed by Ingram (USA, CAN, UK, EU, AU)

Portions of this book previously appeared in *Regina's
Closet: Finding My Grandmother's Secret Journal* (2007)
from Beaufort Books. Used with permission.

Contents

Acknowledgments

My inspiration for this book arrived one fine spring morning during the early days of the coronavirus lockdown. I was sitting at my desk in my writing studio in a somewhat dreamy state, glancing out the window, when a hummingbird arrived on the red flowering plant in my garden. It spent a long time hovering, and it was at that very moment that I decided to write this book. My sense was that the bird arrived at that moment in order to deliver me a message.he unfolding of that message is this book's premise.

So, my first acknowledgment goes to the visiting hummingbird. Her message was loud and clear, and the incident reminded me of the importance of being open to what the universe offers us. Had I not been looking out the window at that very moment, I would have missed seeing it, and this book might not have been brought to fruition. That incident with the hummingbird happened just before my sixty-sixth birthday. In a pleasing parallel, the book's release date coincides with my seventieth birthday.

While it might seem strange to thank a pandemic for an artistic creation, there's no doubt that the lockdown and isolation encouraged me to just sit and write with the deepest focus I'd ever had writing a book. Being my fourteenth book, I speak from experience.

In addition to inspiration, every writer needs a good support system, and I'm very grateful to Simon, my husband and love for more than fifty years. I'm also very grateful for my three children and six grandchildren whose existence has played such a large role in this book. As the family matriarch, subconsciously, I felt pulled to write this book as a gift, as they all are beginning to embark on their own life's journey.

Much of a writer's support system includes publishers and editors who believe in them. Huge thanks to my publisher, Victor Volkman, for once again believing in me and publishing me for the fifth time. Yet again, he believed in my project, even at a time when he was inundated with manuscripts from the masses of individuals, also under isolation, who had plenty to stories and plenty of time to write. He always puts the authors he's already published at the top of his list, but this time I had a lot of competition, as we were all in the same situation.

My long-time, freelance editor, Sharron Dorr, who only takes on one project at a time, once again said she was interested in working with me. I am indebted to her unwavering ability to focus and her meticulous eye for clarity. We worked together on the flow and organization of this book so close to my heart. Her support, enthusiasm, and vision has been instrumental in the completion of the final manuscript.

I am also grateful for Kathleen Lynch, my graphic artist, who once again has created another book cover that I love from the bottom of my heart.

Another integral part of my team is Libby Jordan, whose long-term enthusiasm for my work and creative marketing strategies have been invaluable to me. Our brain-storming sessions have always been illuminating and inspiring.

It would be fair to thank everyone who has crossed my path during this lifetime. A special shout out to some individuals in particular who have touched me with their curiosity, interest, and support during my writing process: Tristine Rainer, Jodi and Johnny Goldberg, Terra Trevor,

Grace Rachow, Charlotte Rains Dixon, Tim Frank, Pam Lancaster, Ljiljana Coklin, Elaina Smolin, and all my many memoir-writing students who feed my soul with their own stories.

I want to thank all my sentient-being ancestors, those who are alive and those who have passed on. As I mention in the book, ancestors also include place, so I want to thank all the places I've visited during the course of my lifetime that have inspired me and that I also call my ancestors.

Last but not least, many thanks to my team of healers who continue to keep me healthy. You know who you are.

I feel extremely blessed and grateful.

Hummingbird

I have fallen in love
with a hummingbird—
the way she arrives each day
at the red flowers outside my studio
and moves among the petals
as if the next has more to offer.

The nectar, oh, it oozes so gently
while other birds nuzzle their beaks
in curiosity.

She might think I'm foolish
to stare at her
in this wonder and amazement,
as she performs so naturally
and I pretend to be writing a new poem
Beseeching her for inspiration.

But, before I can grab her, she's gone
On to the next chore, whatever it might be,
maybe reaching for the heavens or
seeking her ancestral friends who hold answers
from the beyond—which, in the end, is *all* we want.

~ Diana Raab

1 My Story Begins

The story of love is hello and goodbye . . . until we meet again.

~Jimi Hendrix

From an early age, I have been obsessed with storytelling. As an only child growing up in a hardworking family of Eastern European immigrants, I was often alone and left to fend for myself. The peace I found then in reading and writing became a lifelong passion for memoir writing.

This passion intensified when I was ten and began keeping a journal after my maternal grandmother's death—which, because of our deep connection, was an a devastating loss. Afterward, journaling helped me through my troubled adolescence as a hippie in the 1960s, my enforced bed rest when pregnant with my three children, my grief over the losses of more loved ones, and my struggles in coping with two cancer diagnoses. Journaling has also led to my becoming a published author of several books and a writing coach in workshops designed to inspire and help others with their own memoir.

Please feel free to use this book as a guide as you would if attending one of those workshops. In it, as examples of memoir writing I tell stories of some of my familial ancestors and explore my own life in the light of those who have influenced me the most: my grandparents and my parents. I also explore how writing about them—especially my beloved grandmother, Regina—continues to give me hope and inspiration. Various chapters address subjects such as how my grandmother's nurturing caregiving contrasted with that of my mother's narcissistic tendencies; how my grandmother's lessons have helped me through my illnesses and the recent pandemic; how understanding the traumas of our ancestors can give us perspective; how conscious living can help us navigate challenging times; and how gratitude and being in the moment can help us live to the fullest. I also speak about the importance of sharing the stories from our past with future generations: we stand on the shoulders of giants, even though we might not agree with some of their beliefs or with some of the choices they made. And, as always, I write in awareness of the tremendous power words have to shape our lives.

I believe that in addition to having familial ancestors, we also have ancestors of spirit and ancestors of place. However, this book mainly highlights familial or blood-related ancestors. Ancestors of spirit are those who came before us whose calling may be similar to ours. For example, mine would include Florence Nightingdale, Anaïs Nin, and Quan Yin. An intituitve such as Sonia Choquette says that her ancestors of spirit or master teachers include Mother Mary, Jesus Christ, and Mary Magdalene. Connecting with my spirit guides has also inspired different aspects of my life, especially when it comes to how I've been told I am a healer. Ancestors of place are those who came before us who were in a particular place where we were born or lived and with whom we might feel a connection. They could have been neighbors we knew, or maybe someone who built a home we lived in. Even though I don't go into detail about these other types of ancestors, I invite you to explore yours.

At the end of each chapter, I offer a series of reflections or writing prompts to inspire you the reader to identify and explore the significant events of your own life in connection with your own ancestors. You may find stories this way that you want to share, or you may want your writing to be yours and yours alone; the important thing is to write freely with a sense of curiosity and discovery. Feel free to reflect on those questions which particularly resonate with you. There's no need to answer them all, unless you are so inclined.

My hope is that you will find patterns of experience that show you the way forward, just as I have tried to demonstrate through my own memories in this book. By connecting with our ancestors, we obtain access to their wisdom, insights, stories, and guidance, which can help us navigate our own physical and psychological lives.

My grandmother's spirit seems to visit me at crucial times in the form of a hummingbird, symbolic of the sense of joy she bestowed on me. I take great comfort in such visitations and encourage you to search for a symbolic messenger of your own. May your journey be meaningful and also bring you joy and comfort.

2   My Grandmother, My Guide

There is always one moment in childhood when the door opens and lets the future in.

~ Graham Greene

When I was a child, I was often alone and found solace in reading and writing. I loved true stories about real people doing important things. My favorite book was a biography of Florence Nightingale. I loved reading about all the wonderful things she did as the founder of modern nursing. She inspired the healer in me and, eventually, my early career as a registered nurse. Her example gave me a sense of life's infinite possibilities even when my own life seemed narrow and lonely.

Still, my childhood was not always gloomy. My parents, Edward and Eva; my maternal grandparents, Regina and Sam; and I lived in the suburbs of New York City and were often influenced by its cultural sensibilities. From an early age, I was told that I looked like Elizabeth Taylor, but only in adolescence did I understand that it was my sultry green eyes inherited from my father, combined with my dark eyebrows and thick, dark-brown hair inherited from my mother, that bore the resemblance. I had the innate ability to capture people's attention even before I learned to speak. I've continued to have this ability throughout my life, and even though I've never taken advantage of it, I've subconsciously felt blessed.

My bedroom was on the second floor of our pink-shingled, suburban home. My bed had a blue-and-green paisley quilted bedspread with a big, brown cork bulletin board above it featuring photos and poems. Through the window overlooking the backyard, I'd sometimes stare out at the birds to see if they were sending messages. There were all sorts of birds—blue jays, robins, sparrows, and hummingbirds—hovering near the red flowers that Mother had planted and maintained with her green thumb, which unfortunately I did not inherit. As an adult I have been extremely talented in killing the hardiest of house plants.

I lived in that same house until I left for college. I looked out that same bedroom window when, as a teenager, I was having my first LSD trip, which I did in response to my grandfather's death. I remember feeling as if I were having an out-of-body experience and speaking to Grandpa and other loved ones who'd moved into the next realm. That was more than fifty years ago.

Propped up on my childhood bed sat my family of dolls. I cared for them every day, pretending to change, wash, and feed them. My favorite doll was called Tiny Tears, which was a popular doll in the 1950s. She had the magical ability to shed tears from two small holes on either side of the bridge of her nose. This was made possible by feeding her water with a small baby bottle and then pressing her stomach. I tried so hard to make her happy; I couldn't bear to see those tears come from her eyes, which, to me, signaled that she was sad.

For several years when I was young, my maternal grand-parents lived with my parents and me, their bedroom being right beside mine. My grandmother, Regina Reinharz Klein, was my primary caretaker and a huge inspiration. It was she who taught me to type, and I wrote my first short story on the Remington typewriter perched on her vanity. My creativity was set free on that typewriter as I traveled to imaginary places in my mind. Sometimes I read my stories aloud to my dolls.

Caretaking came as naturally to me as it did to my grandmother. She not only taught me how to type and appreciate books, she also taught me how to love and follow my heart and my instincts. Then, when I was ten years old, she died by suicide.

It is often the case that we tend to appreciate people more after they die. They also seem to come more alive when they're gone. Children tend to take experiences more in stride than adults. I didn't grieve openly as my mother did. I grieved quietly in the privacy of my room, with my dolls and my journal. At that tender age, it was impossible fully to understand the permanence of death, but I did understand the deep ache in my heart.

It was then and there that I learned how to console myself through writing. Whenever I wrote, I felt better; I realized how healing it was. Soon afterward, I yearned to share my passion with other neighborhood children, so I organized after-school journaling classes in my backyard. These were also children of hardworking people who didn't have much time for parenting. Many of their young voices remained unheard. Thus, my lessons provided a container for their feelings. As it turned out, they found a lot to write about.

Armed with a stack of black-and-white marbled composition notebooks, pens, and packs of stickers from the local Woolworths, I encouraged the children to decorate and personalize their journals. I told them their journal was their best friend. I suggested they write about their family or whatever concerned them. On some afternoons, especially near the full moon when many of us tend to be more emotional, they wrote nonstop for so long that I had to remind them it was time to go home for dinner. During those days with the neighborhood children, I intuited that storytelling and teaching were my life's calling. It was something I sensed in my heart.

I believe I inherited this deep sense of intuition from my grandmother. In fact, I have often made predications that came true. For the most part, the more we open our spiritual channel, the more things happen.

Years later as an adult, when visiting the spiritual community of Cassadaga near Orlando, Florida, where I lived at the time, I met with an older psychic. My hope was that she could access the additional information I wanted about my grandmother. I shared a black-and-white photo of Grandma in which she was posing with her coifed, short light hair, dark eyebrows, and pencil-thin lips with unexposed teeth. She had high cheekbones highlighted with blush. Her eyes seemed like vortexes of information and pierced right through me.

The rather tall, well-dressed, blonde psychic, also with deep eyes, held the photo and gave it an intense stare. She then looked up at me and stared deep into my own eyes and said, "You know, she's a seer." Her comment stopped me in my tracks. It was as if something I already knew was just confirmed. When someone acknowledges what we already believe, the knowledge somehow becomes even more powerful. Strangely, during my adolescence and early adulthood, I didn't really think much about my grandmother. She was just an ancestor who passed away. I was busy growing up and doing the things teenagers did. Then I got married and began raising three wonderful children of my own.

My life was busy as a writer and mother, fitting in writing between homemaking and chauffeuring my children to and from school and after-school activities. I always wanted to be home for them after school; I never wanted them to be a latchkey child as I had been. At that time, I was lucky enough to have a home office where I could shut the door and do some writing if the kids were busy.

Then, at the age of forty-seven, when everything was going well in my life, there was a huge shift. My teenagers had just finished summer camp, and I was getting them ready to start a new school year. My gynecologist called to say that I had an abnormal mammogram. His shocking phone call divulged that I had ductal carcinoma in situ (DCIS), a precursor of breast cancer, in my right breast. There was no history of cancer in my family. Even so, the diagnosis made me wonder if that had been why my grandmother took her life. I began to feel her intense presence. I believe that I subconsciously called her back because I craved her nurturing and love, something my mother was never capable of providing. In fact, when I phoned my mother to say that I had breast cancer, she responded, "Oh no, I better go get my mammogram!" While it was painful to hear her react in this way, I wasn't surprised because she'd always been self-involved and lacked empathy for me or anyone else.

After my subsequent surgery and recovery, I began to examine and research my grandmother's life at a much deeper level. The cancer diagnosis had made me realize the fragility of life. I spent many hours journaling unfulfilled dreams and realized that I had always wanted to attend graduate school. A few times a year I received *Poets & Writers* magazine, and as I flipped through one, an advertisement captivated my attention. It was for a low-residency MFA degree in writing that offered distance-learning education with a brief on-campus program for weekends or weeks each year. It seemed perfect for someone like me who wanted to minimize my time away from my family. After some discussion with my husband, I applied to and was accepted into the charter class at Spalding University in Louisville, Kentucky. When the time came to do a thesis, which was essentially a writing project, I decided to write the story of Grandma's life interwoven with mine. Based on our relationship for the first ten years of my life, it turned into a memoir entitled *Regina's Closet: Finding My Grandmother's Secret Journal.* My hope in writing the book was to bring her closer to me and also to keep her memory alive.

While researching and writing *Regina's Closet,* I needed help getting more answers about Grandma's life and death. She had had a very small family, and, by the time I was doing the research, many of her relatives had passed away. I met with another psychic who suggested I try to channel with her. She told me to set a time each day to speak with my grandmother and to set up two chairs facing each other in a place where I would not be disturbed. She told me to sit for a few minutes meditating and, when I felt ready, to call on her to join me. Then, the psychic said, we would have a short visitation, and I could ask questions and possibly receive answers. She told me that with practice I would get better at it.

At the same time, I looked at old photographs of my grandmother and tried to dress like her. I wanted to feel as if I were walking in her shoes. I already knew from my mother that Grandma had been a model in her native Austria, always dressing meticulously in fashionable dresses and heels with a matching purse. I had memories of her closet lined up with shoes on a slanted rack on the floor with matching purses hanging on wall hooks.

By trying to become her, I was yearning to infuse myself with my grandmother's wisdom. I tried everything to bring her spirit into my life. For more than three decades, until receiving her journal when I was in my forties, I've had a black-and-white photograph of her perched on my writing desk. I often stare into her big, brown eyes and ask for answers—which she's given me. I've always known that she'd come back to me.

Reflections / Writing Prompts

1. What brought you solace as a child?

2. What does your childhood bedroom look like?

3. What do you know about your maternal and paternal grandparents?

4. Has someone died whom you appreciate more after their passing?

5. Describe the evolution of your religious/spiritual background.

3   When a Loved One Takes Her Life

This life. This night. Your story. Your pain. Your hope. It matters. All of it matters.

~ Jamie Tworkowski

I am a first-generation American. My mother was born in Austria, and my father was born in Germany. They met in New York in the early 1950s. After they married, they worked together in my grandfather's general store in Brooklyn, New York. On Labor Day weekend in 1964, my parents left for their usual day of work while my grandmother stayed home with me in our quiet, working-class neighborhood in Queens. My grandfather was visiting his older sister, Rusza, in Paris.

On that morning, I knocked on Grandma's bedroom door. She didn't answer, so I cracked the door open and got a whiff of her perfume, "Evening in Paris." Out of the corner of my eye, I spotted the sheer white curtains swaying in front of the open window overlooking the street. The air in her room was crisp, and the night's dampness clung to the wooden floor. Grandma's bed was one of two single beds pushed together for her and Grandpa with a single headboard. Her bed was beside the window. Her closet door was closed, and her makeup was spread out on her vanity.

Grandma lay beneath her soft, fringed, Scandinavian wool blanket that she called the warmest blanket in the

world. On her side of the headboard rested Graham
Greene's novel, *The End of the Affair*, a hairbrush, and a
box of Kleenex. An open bottle of pills sat on her
nightstand. Maybe Grandma hadn't been feeling well the
night before and had taken more of her medication than
usual.

"Grandma," I called softly from the doorway. "May I
go to Cindy's?" Cindy was a friend of mine, also ten years
old at the time, who lived around the corner and had a
swimming pool.

Grandma didn't answer. I glanced at my new watch. It
was already ten o'clock. On most days, she was the first
one into the maroon-and-pink-tiled bathroom that all five
of us shared. I walked to the bathroom to see if her
toothbrush was wet. It was dry from (I assumed) having
been used the night before, but her towel, slung sideways
on the towel rack, was still a little damp. The toilet lid was
down, the way she had taught me to leave it. In my fluffy
blue slippers, I returned to Grandma's room and tiptoed
around Grandpa's bed toward hers. I gently tapped her
shoulder.

"Grandma," I repeated, "may I please go swimming at
Cindy's? I'll be back by lunchtime. Promise." Still no
answer. Grandma's face looked pale, and her eyelids were
only partially closed, as if she were about to wake up.

I sensed something was seriously wrong. I tiptoed out of
the room, glancing over my shoulder in the hope that she'd
wake up and answer me. Under the weight of my footsteps,
the wooden floor made creaking sounds, and I trembled
while scurrying to my parents' room at the end of the
hallway. They also had two single beds pushed together
with one headboard. Two pale-pink, electric blankets were
sprawled out on each bed. The beds were unmade, and on
my father's bedside table was an empty plate with crumbs
left from a sandwich he'd eaten the night before. The
oblong wooden table had a glass covering with a display of

family photographs beneath it. One photo that caught my eye was of my grandmother leaning against a tree in our backyard. Her broad smile seemed playful. That's the way I'll always remember her.

I looked at the pink bedside phone but was afraid to pick it up. I glanced at my mother's personal loose-leaf telephone book beside it. Mother was careless about many things, but not her telephone book. This was long before the era of iPhones and similar devices that allow us to store numbers without needing to memorize them. She'd written every number imaginable in this small, loose-leaf book to which she could add numbers. Sometimes, when enough of the entries had become illegible or people had moved so often that she had to do a lot of crossing out, she bought a new book and copied all the numbers into it.

On that Labor Day weekend morning, I knew my mother had gone horseback riding, so I looked up the number of the stable where she kept her horse and dialed it. That day, Mother would be riding in the ring, not in the woods, and the stable boy would certainly pick up the phone. Frantically, I asked to speak to her.

"Mom, I think something's wrong with Grandma," I blurted. "She's not answering when I talk to her."

"*What?*" My mother spoke so loudly that I had to hold the phone away from my ear.

"Mom. Come home. I'm scared," I said, bending my knees and bouncing up and down—an involuntary, agitated gesture—as if I had to go to the bathroom.

"I'm on my way." My mother hung up before I could take my next breath.

For a few moments, I stood staring at the phone, and then I picked it up again to call my father at the store, but he was on his coffee break. I needed to talk to someone. I was petrified and intuited that something was not right. I wondered what to do. Should I wait in the living room, or on the front lawn, or at Grandma's side? I was afraid to go back into her room. Had she awakened, she would have called me.

I ran downstairs and then ran right back up again, feeling lost in my own home. I flew into my room, grabbed the Tiny Tears doll off my bed, and then scurried back downstairs, stumbling in my haste down the last two steps.

I waited near the living-room window, walking in circles like a cat chasing its tail. I hugged my doll so tightly that she wet her pants. The water I'd poured into the hole in her back to make her tears must have leaked out. I didn't want to go back upstairs for another diaper. I was too scared.

Finally, I settled in the bay window with the padded pillow beside the front door. I sat cuddled up on its ledge as I had so many times before, waiting for my parents to drive in at the end of the day. My nose was glued to the cool glass. This time, more than ever, I was eager for an adult to come home.

Soon, an ambulance siren stirred the ordinarily quiet residential neighborhood, and I watched as a fire truck pulled up in front of our house facing the wrong way against traffic. From the other direction came another set of flashing lights and a siren. It was a police car, which came roaring up and stopped in the street. The policeman flung his car door open toward the curb and dashed up to the house. Terror grabbed me amid all the commotion. Three firemen followed the policeman and, before I knew it, strangers were invading our home.

My mother arrived from the stable, and my father returned from work in his pink Chevrolet, the one that matched the house. My dad had been so happy the day I was born that, within a week of my birth, he had painted the shingled house pink and bought a pink car.

Uniformed paramedics, their blue, short-sleeved shirts rolled up to reveal bulging muscles, arrived next and bounded up the four steps to our front door. My mother loved gardening. There were always beautiful flowers in the garden, and a flowering plant usually graced the kitchen table. To get to the front door, the men had to pass the Japanese cherry-blossom tree that Mother had planted on the front lawn the year I was born. It wasn't in bloom yet, and its bare branches echoed the coldness I felt inside. The men brushed by the dying rhododendron bushes on either side of the steps and flung open the screen door. When they saw me at the windowsill, one of them quickly asked, "Who's sick here?" I pointed in the direction of the wooden stairs leading to my grandmother's bedroom, and they ran past me as if I were part of the décor. I felt like a stranger in my own home.

I stood up and followed them.

"You stay right there, little girl," the last paramedic in the group turned and said as I started to climb the stairwell to see Grandma.

Standing at the bottom of the stairs looking up, I fiddled with my clammy hands and crossed my legs, afraid to run to the bathroom because I might miss something. The fear I felt about what was going on made me feel as if I had to pee.

Mother came in through the front door, rushed up to me, kissed my forehead, and then took off after the paramedics. I still remember the lingering fragrance of her perfume. My father, who tended to become queasy in medical situations, stood outside the house speaking with the ambulance driver, looking ashen and nervous. After a while, he started pacing on the sidewalk. He clearly didn't want to be a part of the commotion that was happening inside. In those days, many adults smoked cigarettes, especially when under stress or in social settings. But I didn't see him light up. He must have been too nervous to even think about smoking.

What were they doing to my beloved grandmother? Were they lifting her up, trying to get her to walk? It never crossed my mind that she might have died. I just thought she wasn't feeling well, so they'd be taking her to the hospital. I knew about hospitals because, when I was seven years old I'd had a bad sore throat, and my parents told me I would have to have my tonsils out. The best part of the surgery was being allowed to have all the ice cream I wanted afterward. Now I wondered if Grandma would have the same experience. Death was rarely discussed in those days.

I ventured over to the base of the stairs. My eyes fixed on the mirror on the linen-closet door at the top of the landing. Once I'd seen a ghost in that mirror on my way to the bathroom in the middle of the night. It was a white, clown-like figure with onyx dots for eyes. It spooked me, and I scooted back to bed. After that night, I always made sure my parents left the hall light on. I didn't want to see any more ghosts.

Soon, I spotted two paramedics grasping both ends of a stretcher on which lay my grandmother with straps across her body holding her in place. With quick and urgent steps, they transported her down the steep stairs leading to the front door. I wondered what would happen if they slipped and Grandma went flying.

As the men and stretcher approached the bottom of the stairs where I was still standing, I noticed my grandmother's stiffness and how her eyes were still closed. I inched close to her and whispered, "Grandma." I didn't realize this was my last hope of ever hearing her voice. I felt the eyes of one of the paramedics on me as he tossed me a sympathetic glance.

My mother followed behind and gave me a rushed hug. "You stay home with Daddy," she said. "That'll be the best."

"Will Grandma be okay?" I asked, looking for solace in her dark brown eyes, but there was none. Many years later, when I found my grandmother's death certificate, I learned that she had taken an overdose of Valium, a medication the family physician prescribed for her anxiety and depression.

~ ~ ~

After Grandma died, my life changed drastically. When alive, she had taught me that everything is impermanent, and that life and death are a normal part of the circle of life. Thus, she taught me the importance of living each day to its fullest and as if it were my last.

While she didn't mention or refer to her own death, in retrospect, I wonder if she was preparing me for it. I think that by teaching me that everything is impermanent, she was also teaching me the importance of gratitude and of living in the present moment. When we live in the present, there's a greater tendency to be grateful. I was thankful for each moment Grandma had spent with me, teaching me how to type and inspiring my future passion for journaling.

My parents didn't tell me how she died, but I do remember that Mother became very sad. In her grief, she began dressing only in black. For most of my early adolescence, she lay curled in a fetal position on the vinyl sofa in our den. I'd often come home from school and hear her crying in agony. Instead of being comforted, I wound up doing the comforting. I'd bring her cold glasses of water and dry her eyes with tissues. She never had the words to explain her feelings. Now, at ninety-three, she still has difficulty expressing her deepest sentiments. Her way of expressing herself was through tears, which inspired me at a young age to use my imagination and write stories and poems in my journals.

In fact, my journaling practice began after Grandma died. My mother, in struggling with her own grief, realized she was emotionally unavailable to me and thought having a journal would help me. As an English major in college, she'd always kept a journal. So, three generations of women—my grandmother, my mother, and I—have all been all journal keepers. A few days after Grandma's funeral, Mother bought me a Khalil Gibran journal from our neighborhood bookstore.

"I know you loved and cherished your grandmother, and I know how much you miss her," Mother said. "I thought you'd like to keep a journal in the same way she did. Maybe it will help you cope with losing her. You can start by writing her a letter." Then she handed the journal over to me one evening while I was lying on my bed reading, in my room with the colorful Tiffany light hanging on the ceiling.

It was the perfect gift for the budding writer inside of me. On the top of each page was an inspirational quote from Gibran. On some days, I just freely wrote whatever was on my mind, but on other days, I needed more inspiration, and so his words inspired my own.

For hours on end, I sat writing on the floor of my walk-in closet with clothes hanging in my face. Journaling seemed to be an ideal way for me to deal with my loss. It was the 1960s, and psychotherapy wasn't widely advocated or available for adults or children. If it had been, maybe my grandmother might not have taken her life.

Reflections / Writing Prompts

1. If you have known someone who has taken their life, discuss what you know about it.

2. Think about a transformative moment in your childhood. What happened?

3. Describe what healing methods you have turned to during challenging times.

4. Write a letter to a loved one who has passed on.

5. Explain your first experience with death and how it affected you.

4   Visitations

Some people are your relatives but others are your ancestors,
and you choose the ones you want to have as your ancestors.
You create yourself out of those values.

~ Ralph Ellison

Each day a hummingbird visits the garden outside my
writing studio. She loves the red trumpet vine that bears
delicious nectar. She hovers in the center of the flower for a
few seconds, levitates, and then moves on to the next vine.
Her movements are so quick that I have to keep a close eye
so as not to miss her before she flies away. She seems to
have a lot to do over the course of her day as she bestows
her magic on plants and other sentient beings.

It's been said that those who were close to you before
they died commonly send messages in the form of bird
spirit guides. Hummingbirds, in particular, resonate at a
high vibration, which makes them more connected to the
spiritual realm. They're also joyful reminders and tend to
open our hearts and make us smile. They're referred to as
messengers from the heavens because they often show up
when people grieve the loss of a loved one. In this way,
they can also be healing. If you ever watch a hummingbird,
you'll notice that it can come to a complete stop when
traveling at high speed. Also, their movements are often in
the shape of an infinity sign; thus their connection to
eternity.

Some Native Americans believe that the presence of hummingbirds brings unconditional love and harmony. The Aztecs, in particular, viewed hummingbirds as brave and courageous fighters. They also believed hummingbirds to be immortal, connecting us with our ancestors. The fact is that, whenever one appears, it's sometimes viewed as a visitation from an ancestor or a manifestation of a dead person's spirit.

In *Ancestral Medicine: Rituals for Personal and Family Healing* (2017), Dr. Daniel Foor states that connecting with our ancestors is beneficial for our psychological and physical health. Not only can it boost our confidence and intellectual performance, it also makes us aware of family predispositions that can benefit us and future generations, in addition to helping to promote forgiveness. Further, it encourages introspection and can bring clarity about our life purpose. Those who are connected with their ancestors often feel more supported and comfortable in their skin.

Foor (2017) has described how connecting with ancestors can help heal intergenerational trauma or family dysfunction. The fact is that when you are a child of someone who has experienced tremendous trauma, those memories can become yours. It's almost unfathomable, but children can live with memories of events that never even happened to them. Many studies are emerging on the significance of *epigenetics*—the study of how behavior and environment can alter the way one's genes work—and we now know that there's a connection between parental trauma before conception and epigenetic alterations that are present both in the parent and in their children.

Many intuitive individuals believe that hummingbirds are the greatest proof of messages from heaven. When settling down to sleep at night, these birds have the ability to lower their metabolism to the minimum necessary to sustain life. To conserve energy, their metabolism comes to an almost complete standstill. They can also easily travel backward, which reminds us that it's okay to look to our past and connect with memories of loved ones who have passed away.

I'm quite sure that my grandmother, who died in 1964 at the age of sixty-one, frequently visits me in the form of a hummingbird. She sends messages of love and offers me ongoing protection. She reminds me that everything is temporary and of how important it is to enjoy my time here on Earth. She tells me that her time here was too short and that being my grandma and caretaker was one of her greatest joys and accomplishments. She reminds me to rise above the everyday, rudimentary concerns of life and look at the larger picture. She says that, with love, we can accomplish almost anything, and a life without love is an empty one.

If we pay attention, the universe has a way of sending us signs. I believe that if we pay attention, we receive signs from the departed that help show us the way. Some people call these entities guardian angels, while others refer to them as spirit guides. They visit in different forms, so you must open your heart to the secret messages being sent your way.

I am not the only one who receives messages from the departed through birds. Birds are like omens. Some people say they're a source of spiritual inspiration. After all, like angels, they have wings. This makes sense to me, as birds are able to fly close to the heavens and gather wisdom and messages to bring back to us here on Earth. Over the years, I've learned to be mindful of these messages. I've become more attentive during this chapter of my life, my sixties—the same decade of life in which my grandmother died. So, whenever a bird visits me, I tune right in.

My father, Edward, is another ancestor who has visited me. Dad was short in stature—standing about five foot nine—but he had a big personality, always with a smile on his face exposing his perfectly aligned, capped teeth. He had a large forehead and black, thinning, slicked-back hair. He loved making jokes, and his loving nature thrived on making others happy.

Living through the Holocaust from the age of fifteen to twenty, my father lost his parents and youngest brother in Dachau's gas chambers, so a growing family became very important to him. His life mission after emigrating to the United States at the end of World War II was to bring as much peace as possible into his life and into the lives of his loved ones. Decades later, he was especially joyful when he was the first grandparent to meet his grandbaby. He was a retail toy salesman and yearned to start bestowing the latest toys on his first grandchild.

My father died more than thirty years after Grandma. Now he visits me as a dove, symbolizing peace, which I need during challenging times. I was navigating tough waters while raising three teenagers and facing—and then surviving—two cancer journeys.

Even though my father left this physical plane so long ago, I believe that the dove's visits are his way to remind me of his presence. He continues to remind me to seek peace for myself and for those I love.

When my grandmother and father were alive, they provided me with unconditional love, and they continue to do so on their visitations. They don't give me direct, detailed instructions. Rather, they support and guide me on my life journey. I sometimes feel their presence over my right shoulder as if an energy were coming through—a physical sensation such as tingling or chills in the upper part of my body. Once in a while, I feel their presence when one of my extremities falls asleep. Sometimes I hear Dad giving me advice or telling me that everything will be okay.

My grandmother's messages come to me in other subtle ways—an unexpected bird, an out-of-the-blue phone call, a certain book falling off my shelf, a certain song playing on the radio, a light flickering in the house, or her whispering into my right ear. It might only be a word or two, but it's usually enough to relay an important message, much as the hummingbirds seem to do.

This connection with birds can also be a way to connect with our own souls.

My mother was in her thirties when Grandma died. That's too young to lose a mother. In the wake of this misfortune, perhaps during her long hours of birdwatching my young mother was searching for her lost soul. She seemed empty, as if an essential part of herself were missing. Grief dimmed her aura. As James Joyce said in *Portrait of the Artist as a Young Man* (1916), "Each lost soul will be a hell unto itself, the boundless fire raging in its very vitals."

While Grandma had been a "seer," my mother was more of a new soul. (I think the "seer" characteristic skipped a generation.) But she was a keen observer. After my grandmother died, I'd sometimes find Mother sitting in the yard, birdwatching, remarking on their varieties and behaviors. She had all sorts of bird feeders, some elevated on poles and others hanging from trees. Her passion was to study what food each species of bird liked, and she'd fill the feeders accordingly. In the winter, she filled the feeders with suet cakes embedded with assorted bird seed. "The fat helps them keep warm," she told me.

Unfortunately, since I moved her into an assisted-living facility five years ago, my ninety-three-year-old mother has lost her *joie de vivre* and no longer expresses interest in birds or in the horses she rode until she was eighty. As an only child, I'm the one who makes all the decisions about Mother's care. I insisted she stop riding when she was eighty because she'd had a terrible fall and ended up in the ICU with a concussion. Now, cognitive decline has begun to set in, as is often the case when we are no longer able to tap into our passions. But her small, six-hundred-square-foot apartment at her assisted-living facility has photos of her riding her horse on each wall.

Like a hummingbird who can fly backward, my mother had a tendency to look back on life rather than to look forward. She has always been obsessed with the past and often lingered there. She had difficulty adapting to not having her mother around. It was as if she was unable to function or make any decisions, whether it had to do with making dinner or what to do in her spare time.

Often depressed and tired, my mother slept for long stretches on the weekend and on her days off. She had worked at my grandparents' general store, Klein's on Broadway in Brooklyn, when younger and then as a unit coordinator in the local hospital during the last twenty-five years of her working life. She was never a good cook or housekeeper—tasks she suddenly had to take on when my grandmother passed. Mother detested them. On the days she worked, she'd do the grocery shopping on her way home from work. Much like Europeans in those times, she'd buy only enough food for one day.

After Grandma died, our household consisted of just four people—my mother, my father, my grandfather, and I. In order to do the domestic work my grandmother had done, Mother shortened her working hours outside the home, which I suspect she resented. By nature, she wasn't a very nurturing woman, a characteristic exacerbated by the depression brought on by losing her mother. So, when my primary caretaker was gone, I felt abandoned because my grandfather, father, and mother were all gone much of the time—if Mother wasn't working, she was riding her horse or meeting with friends.

As a result, I became quite independent. It seems I was destined to be a survivor. In my youth, I survived the loss of my primary caretaker while also surviving being the only daughter of a mother with narcisstic tendencies. According to Mark Epstein in his book, *Thoughts Without a Thinker,*

(1995), "When a child, seeking contact with another person rather than just instinctual gratification, comes up against a narcissistic parent, too preoccupied with her own search to attend to the child's, the child is left with a feeling of absence that becomes the seed of her own fear and insecurity" (p. 37). There's no doubt that this is what happened to me.

Years later, I became a two-time cancer survivor. I've intuitively known how to care for myself by surrounding myself with those who love me. I've sought good and lighthearted people. At home, I was often the mediator between two warring parents, so I tried to infuse all other realms of my life with calm.

I began meditating in the early 1970s before it was trendy. I was selective about my friends, and it took time for me to trust people. Losing my grandmother had hurled me into a barbed cycle of fear. As a teen, when boyfriends broke up with me, I remained locked in trauma long after my friends in similar situations had moved on. I was constantly in a state of self-protection, afraid that through death, abandonment, or both, I would be left alone.

Over the years, I've come to believe that difficult moments of our childhoods can continue to trigger us for the rest of our lives. Sometimes when I felt unloved or reprimanded, I'd shut down. Five years after my grandmother died, I had a heated disagreement with my mother. I can't recall what she said, but I do remember it was the first time I realized that our worldviews were in complete opposition. She had a way of diminishing my self-esteem and making me feel empty inside. For example, she'd ridicule me in front of others.

People have often asked how it is possible that I'm her daughter, as our energies are completely different. My mother's negativity often made people feel deflated. In contrast, I have been a positive person who made people feel good about themselves. As Maya Angelou wisely said,

"People will forget what you said, people will forget what you did, but people will never forget how you made them feel."

The fact is, as children, we don't initially realize the impact of crises such as losing a loved one or learning that we weren't wanted. Dr. Bessel van der Kolk, in *The Body Keeps Score* (2014), says that if we feel safe and loved, our brains become specialized in play, exploration, and cooperation. On the other hand, if you are scared and feeling unwanted, you will be dealing with feelings of fear and a sense of abandonment.

It took many years for me to feel safe and loved. The first time I felt that way was when I was eighteen and met the man who became my husband. That was in 1972, and now, more than fifty years later, he's still not let me down. I always felt he'd protect me when my mother said and did hurtful things—for example, calling me two weeks before my wedding day to say she wouldn't pay for my wisdom teeth removal, even though she had the money to do so. Or saying she wasn't interested in helping me choose my wedding gown, even though she really liked my husband and his family. My husband disliked her for how intentionally mean and insensitive she was, especially to me. I suppose the silver lining is that I became an empath.

For the most part, children and young adults take things in stride; but sometimes, if they have a difficult time expressing their feelings, their bodies give them messages. After my grandmother died, my parents began fighting a lot. It was difficult to watch and impossible to process. I believe my childhood asthma might have signaled that I was stressed by circumstances at home. According to the Cleveland Clinic, traumatized children have shown asthma rates fifty times higher than their peers. As an adolescent, I hung out with teens who took illegal drugs, and I stayed away from home as much as possible. I felt adrift, searching for a way to reconnect with Grandma. Now I'm left to wonder if the hummingbird visitations are a way to make that connection. Are her messages a way for me to heal from my grief both over losing her and over not being wanted by my mother?

Reflections / Writing Prompts

1. Write about an incident from your childhood that transformed you.

2. Who in your life, alive or deceased, provided you with the most unconditional love? Describe how they displayed their love.

3. Discuss the first time you lost someone whom you loved deeply.

4. Write about an experience you've had with a visitation from a deceased loved one.

5. Write about a book or books that changed your worldview or perception.

5   My Grandfather and I

The closing years of life are like the end of a masquerade party, when the masks are dropped.

~ Cesare Pavese

Often when a loved one dies, we try to replace that person with someone else. Sometimes the decision to do so is conscious, and other times it's not. Because my grandfather also lived with us when I was a child, it was quite natural for me to try to replace my grandmother's presence with his. Having him in my life and nurturing my regular journaling practice were two powerful healing forces for me.

My grandfather told me stories about all his travels after emigrating to the United States from Austria in the late 1930s. In the few weeks after Grandma died, he spent a lot of time with me. I believe he was trying to distract me from missing her when my parents were at work. He graciously invited me into his world.

In fact, if there was a bright spot in the loss of my grandmother, it was that I grew closer to my grandfather. I didn't realize it at the time, but she had kept me isolated from him. Forty years after her passing, I found personal documents in her closet. Included in them was one of her journals, from which I learned that, in the few years before her suicide, even though my grandparents had lived together in the same house with all of us, they were legally separated. Legal paperwork I discovered in her closet revealed that my grandfather had been physically abusive toward her. Did she prevent me from seeing or spending time with him to protect me?

I never saw the abusive side of him; but once, when Grandma was still alive, I came down the stairs leading to the living room and saw my grandparents yelling at one another, each standing on opposite sides of the room. In her right hand, she held an empty, green drinking glass. She looked as if she were ready to throw it at my grandfather. When she saw me approach, she quickly hid the glass behind her back. Even as a child, I had the ability to sense the energy in a room. It was always easy for me to pick up vibes. At that moment, I felt some awful energy. I sensed something wrong was going on between my grandparents, and I knew it wasn't my place to witness it. I scurried back upstairs and locked myself in my room until my parents came home from work. After reading my grandmother's journal, I suspect she might have been imitating what she learned from her own mother about how to behave in a marriage, as she wrote that she had often heard her parents argue. I can only assume. We can't help but learn by example.

As children, we don't usually question adult relationships. However, there were times when I intuitively felt things weren't right between my grandparents. My family wasn't communicative about their feelings, but they certainly gave off vibes that I was able to decipher at a young age. As an adult, I wonder if Grandma fabricated the story about Grandpa striking her to find her way out of an unhappy marriage. Would she do such a thing? Who was the hummingbird and who was the dragon? I'll never know.

With me, my grandfather was a gentleman who introduced me to the cultural wonders of New York City. For about twenty years, until his untimely passing, he and I were quite close. So, I'm left wondering—are we all chimeras and shapeshifters who exist as different beings in different spaces and moments and with different people? A hummingbird one moment, a dragon the next?

Many of us have different personas and wear different masks at different times. Only those close to us truly know us. My mother was a master of masks. To the outside world, she was charming, vivacious, and joyous, but at home, she was somber and depressed. I wonder if she inherited this trait from my grandfather, who also wore two masks. He was abusive toward my grandmother yet gentle and caring to me and others. Many people have two masks: an inside mask that we keep for our loved ones and an outside mask for the world to see.

As an avid reader and longtime observer of character, I understand the appeal of masks. A mask portrays emotions or serves as protection. In the sport of falconry, a falcon is fitted with a mask called a "trapping hood" to calm and protect it in scary situations. My grandfather's "trapping hood" could have been his way of protecting himself from expressing rage in public. It calmed him and enabled him to act like a gentleman.

If we feel unloved by others, we might hide behind the mask of anger. If we're afraid, we might hide under a mask that antagonizes others by insulting them or putting them down. If we're insecure about our perceived status, we might hide behind the mask of name-dropping—talking about celebrities or important figures. If we're insecure or unsure of our power, we might hide under the "tough-person" mask. If we're in a bad or difficult relationship, we might wear the mask signifying that everything is okay. Apparently, this was the mask my grandparents wore.

At the end of May 1980, while I was preparing for my nursing-licensure exams, my mother phoned me in

Montreal, where my husband and I had moved after we married in 1977.

"Deedle, your grandfather came in from his walk around the block earlier today and complained of a bad stomachache. He went to his internist who immediately sent him to the hospital emergency room. They diagnosed him with a ruptured aortic aneurysm. I'm so upset, Diana. He needs immediate surgery," she said tearfully and with more emotion than I'd ever heard her express.

I was torn about where to be or what to do. "Mom, what shall I do? This is so hard. I want to be in two places at once."

"I think you should stay in Montreal and take your nursing-licensure exams. Why don't you visit him next week when he gets home? You'll be more help to me then, too."

My grandfather was on the operating room table for at least twelve hours—a lengthy surgery for an eighty-three-year-old man. As a neophyte registered nurse who'd already done a rotation in the operating room of a teaching hospital, I wondered if they'd used my grandfather's medical predicament for teaching purposes by having the residents attend to him. In those days, patients weren't savvy about this sort of thing. We would never have thought of questioning a doctor's suggestion. Plus, there was no Internet on which to learn about such things. We were forced to trust our health-care team. Since then, for my multiple surgeries, I've insisted that no residents get their scalpels near me.

To my enduring dismay, I never got the chance to kiss my grandfather goodbye. On Sunday, June 22, 1980—coincidentally, the day after Grandma's birthday—my grandfather died in the intensive-care unit of surgical complications. This was sixteen years after my grandmother's passing.

My grandfather never spoke to me about my grandmother's death. I don't think he wanted to say anything about her that would hurt me, so he wisely chose not to say anything at all. In this way, I was left with only good memories of her, and the bitterness between my grandparents never interfered with my relationship with either of them. I feel lucky to have benefited from two wonderful although completely independent relationships with each of my grandparents, and the memories of them will live with me forever. They gave me an additional perspective on life that contributed to my own confidence and success. They also instilled in me awareness of the important role that grandparents can play in a child's life, which I've carried with me into my own grandparenthood. There is something to be said about just connecting and having fun together. There aren't as many rules as there are with parents, and grandparents tend to spoil their grandchildren.

Until his sudden illness and death, my grandfather was a tall, good-looking, thick-white-haired gentleman who swam in the ocean a few times a week. He said salt water was good for the soul. He, too, had been a model in Vienna, and he was a sharp dresser who, on most days, wore finely tailored business suits. A quiet man, after a long day of work at the store he and Grandma owned, he'd sit in the living room alone, watching the evening news on his twelve-inch television that sat on the glass coffee table between the two yellow twisted velour sofas. From a child's perspective, Grandpa minded his own business.

I had a difficult time dealing with the loss of my grandfather, my last grandparent. I felt lucky to have danced with him at my wedding three years earlier. In some ways I was prepared for his death because, a few years before I got married, he had had a heart attack that landed him in the coronary-care unit. I was terrified of losing him. That night was the first time I took an LSD trip as a way to cope with the possibility of the loss.

Many years later after I became a grandmother, I dove into a deep depression. I tried many holistic curatives but was unable to pull myself out of it. My depression wasn't caused by anything external, other than the possibility that I'd need treatment one day for multiple myeloma, but that was not impending at that time. Everything was basically going well in my life: I had a terrific marriage with three great adult children and five grandchildren, and I was writing a lot of articles and poems.

The depression came on in the middle of the coronavirus pandemic; for help, I phoned my shaman friend who lived in Arizona. The Arizona healer and I had known each other for more than fifteen years, and, in many ways, he was like the brother I never had—or maybe even better. He had a way of pulling me out of the darkness. He had a great sense of humor and was able always to put life's experiences in the proper perspective.

During our phone session, I told him what I was going through and that I didn't want to end up dead by suicide as my grandmother had. I also told him that I had spoken with a psychiatrist who had given me a test and ascertained that I had moderate to severe depression. When the psychiatrist said I needed an antidepressant, I refused. He told me that in addition to talk therapy, the only other option was to exercise and get into a sweat for at least an hour each day. As a sixty-seven-year-old, I felt daunted.

I told my shaman that, like my grandmother, I no longer felt needed by or important to my children, who had become parents themselves. My husband had retired and was very busy with his own projects and being alone. I was starting to feel the loneliness of being an only child. The shaman reminded me of the importance of my being and of all I had to offer the universe as a sage, a writer, and a writing teacher. He told me that he would not accept my choice of suicide. He suggested I visit him and his wife and take a journey to get me out of the rut. That was the second time in my life that I did psilocybin. Thankfully, with the couple's guidance during the four days we were together, combined with the medicine (psilocybin), I was healed. I suppose that story will be another book one day.

Briefly, what came out of that experience was the insight that in my heart I was holding all my father's pain as a Holocaust survivor. The struggle wasn't even mine, but for all these years, I'd been holding it in my heart for him. My body held the memory. In fact, when I was under the influence of psilocybin, I actually went through the Holocaust with him, and a deep anger emerged at all the Nazis who had forced all the Jews to walk onto those trains and into those ovens. It was crazy that my subconscious was holding all this pain. The medicine led me from the darkness into the light, and I am forever grateful. The experience also gave me the chance to reflect on my ancestors and their constant effect on my life and the lives of my children. They are all with us, in our DNA, and watching over us.

Over the years, I've often thought about all the memorable times I'd spent with my grandfather, the oldest ancestor I knew. When I was a teenager with a rebellious streak dealing with the challenges of being a hippie in the 1960s, each year for my winter holiday my grandfather and I vacationed at his rental apartment in Miami, Florida. Each Sunday when we were home in Queens, Grandpa and I took the subway to New York City. His favorite spot was Stouffer's restaurant on top of the building at 666 Fifth Avenue. One trip when I was about twelve really stands out. I'd asked him if we could have our outing on Friday instead of Sunday that week because I had an important paper due on Monday.

"Are you sure you can't go on Sunday?" he asked, sounding disappointed. He, too, cherished our outings together.

"I'm sure, Grandpa. It's the end of the semester, and it's an important assignment. Mom is going to take me to the library to finish my research."

"I have an idea," he said. "How about we go to the library in the city? That'll be an adventure."

"That big one with all the stairs?"

"No, that's the main library. It's too busy there. Let's try the one on 55th Street, directly across the street from the Museum of Modern Art."

That museum was one of my grandfather's favorites, particularly because it was up the street from Stouffer's restaurant.

"Okay. Let's do that, Grandpa. I'll pack my books."

I felt so mature doing an assignment in a big-city library. My grandfather introduced me to the librarian and then sat patiently reading *The New York Times* in the periodical section. After I completed my assignment, we went to Stouffer's, where the waitress teased me about being my grandfather's young girlfriend. In those days it was cute, but things have changed, and these days her comment would not have been taken well.

Occasionally on our outings, my grandfather surprised me with theater tickets for a Broadway show. Our relationship revolved around those weekend outings and going clothes shopping together. I sensed the joy it gave him to help me choose my wardrobe. I also trusted his taste. As a former model, he was savvy about styles and was particular about the materials chosen by the designers. Each summer, he visited England and always brought back my wardrobe for the new school year. Receiving my grandfather's undivided attention was a vital and positive part of my adolescence. He became my best friend and grounded me as I struggled with adolescent angst and the chaotic world that surrounded me growing up in New York in the 1960s.

The summer I turned seventeen, Grandpa took me to Paris to visit his sister, Rusza. We went on long walks, and then we'd sit for hours in the busy cafés. His favorite one was Café de la Paix. Those early childhood experiences fostered my love for people watching and thus a future life as a writer.

~ ~ ~

A few years after my grandfather died and during my nursing residency in Montreal, I had an interesting encounter with a female patient who, in so many ways, reminded me of my grandmother. While I didn't find it significant at the time, looking back, I recall that she had a photograph of a hummingbird on her hospital bedside table. I remember remarking on its iridescent colors. She told me she loved those birds and had special feeders in her yard with sweetened red water that attracted them.

At the time, there was a nursing shortage in the psychiatric unit, so I was asked to leave the cardiac unit and help in that other one. On that day, I was given only one "client," as we called them. We called this patient "Mrs. G." because she had a long Polish name that nobody could pronounce.

That day began with morning rounds, which involved the doctors, nurses, and nursing students going from room to room to visit all the clients on the unit. The head nurse or physician in chief summarized the reason for the patient's hospitalization and their current status. Sometimes a patient's condition evoked a discussion, while other times the clan moved quickly from one room to the next.

We entered Mrs. G.'s room, and I stood at the back of the line. When I moved forward and saw her, I was stunned beyond words. I thought I was looking into the eyes of my grandmother. Her blonde hair had dark roots that matched her well-defined eyebrows. She was applying lipstick, and her mannerisms were Grandma's. She traced her mouth with a lip liner, making her lips appear larger, and came to a well-defined point in the middle of her top lip.

"I feel naked without my lipstick," Grandma used to tell me, and I sensed that Mrs. G. held similar sentiments.

She finished applying her lipstick and sat in bed, dressed in a pink skirt and matching floral blouse. When I asked why she was not wearing a hospital gown, I was told that she insisted on using her own clothing, something Grandma would also have requested. I watched this striking, sixty-something blonde woman staring out the window. Her blue eyes emanated intelligence, pain, and reflection. I wondered if my grandmother's eyes showed the same pain before she took her life.

The doctor in charge introduced himself to Mrs. G. and asked how she was doing. She muttered something softly, to which the doctor barely responded. It felt dismissive to me, as if her answer really didn't matter. I thought about how Mrs. G. and my grandmother might have simply needed someone to talk to and about how there are more talkers in the universe than listeners. We then all convened in the corridor and discussed Mrs. G.'s case.

"Mrs. G. has been depressed for many months," said the doctor in charge. "Her family admitted her to the hospital because she tried to commit suicide by taking an overdose of her blood-pressure pills."

The mention of the word *suicide* made me feel as if a dagger had been plunged deep inside my heart. I was glad I'd gulped down a bowl of cereal that morning. It helped ease the sudden nausea.

One doctor asked the nurse about the medications that Mrs. G. was taking. Another inquired about her treatment. After all the questions were answered, the troop of nurses and doctors moved on to the next client. I hung at the back of the group and then stepped inside the room again to get a better look at Mrs. G.

Unfortunately, she had drifted into sleep, or was pretending to do so, and was oblivious to my presence. I don't know if there actually were sheer curtains swaying near the window or if my mind put them there as I thought about the last time I'd seen my grandmother's face in her bedroom beside mine in my childhood home.

The head nurse approached me and whispered, "Mrs. G. attempted to kill herself the night she found her husband, twenty years her junior, sleeping with another woman." Then she stepped out of the room.

I gasped.

I couldn't leave the room. I felt a gravitational pull toward Mrs. G. I nudged myself closer to her bed in the small, private room with the window overlooking the hospital roof. I carefully drew the privacy curtains around her bed and sat on the vinyl chair beside her. Part of me wanted to wake her—to hear her voice, her tone, her story. Another part of me was petrified. I stared until I heard the head nurse's footsteps outside the curtain. She poked her head in through the opening.

"Are you okay?" she asked.

I nodded, afraid to admit how the woman resembled my grandmother—in appearance and mannerisms and deed. I thought about the possibility of removing myself from the unit because I had a family history of suicide. On the other hand, with my background I felt as if I *should* be there. It was strange being in the company of a woman who so closely resembled Grandma. When looking at her photographs, I'd look deep into her eyes, wondering if I'd ever find out why she killed herself. I stopped when I realized I never would. Still, I'm comforted by the knowledge that we had such a powerful and deep love for each other. For now, this would have to be enough.

My grandparents never spoke about each other to me. In discussions with each of them, whenever I mentioned the other's name, whomever I was speaking with didn't respond but sat with a blank affect, similar to the vibe I'd picked up from Mrs. G. Their silence told a story. My childhood was filled with ambiguity, especially when it came to the relationships of my parents and grandparents. In a sense, everyone came together in their love for me. I was the glue that held the family together, something I continue to do now as I've become a grandmother myself.

That evening, when I returned home from the hospital, I pulled out my journal to write about the day's experience. I glanced up at the framed quote hanging above my desk, which is from François Mauriac's book, *The Desert of Love* (1960): "We are, all of us, molded and remolded by those who have loved us, and though that love may pass, we remain none the less their work—a work that very likely they do not recognize, and which is never exactly what they intended."

Reflections / Writing Prompts

1. Have you lost a loved one whom you tried to replace with someone else?

2. Are you familiar with a story about someone that emerged only after they died?

3. What were your superpowers when you were younger? What are they now?

4. What were your passions as a child, and who inspired them?

5. What genetic traits did you inherit from a beloved parent or grandparent?

6   Cancer, Quarantine, and Intuition

Intuition doesn't tell you what you want to hear; it tells you what you need to hear.

~ Sonia Choquette

I have cancer again, but not breast cancer this time. We are in the midst of a pandemic. It's December 2020, and I'm preparing to meet my new oncologist. For the past fourteen years, my former oncologist has been following my smoldering multiple myeloma—a cancer of the plasma cells in the bone marrow—called "smoldering," meaning that I have no symptoms except abnormal blood work. But now he has returned home to his native Canada, having connected me with a new oncologist in a different hospital with whom he'd done research. He did warn me that there are differing approaches to this disease and that the new doctor's treatment might be more aggressive.

I'm getting ready for my first on-site visit following one telemedicine call. Simon, my husband of nearly forty-five years, said he'd drive me. He worked hard to protect me from any harm that others might bestow on me and also protected me from getting depressed about this second type of cancer. As a retired engineer, slender and standing over six feet, his positive and grateful life view has helped me survive many of life's turbulent moments. While he had a red Afro when we met before college, now at seventy he's balding with salt-and-pepper hair. He laughs and says marriage has inspired the hair loss, but I do my research and learn that it's all about genetics.

People often ask me, what are the secrets of a long-term marriage? My answer is always the same: inspire one another to follow dreams, have open communication, and laugh. In her book *Women Rowing North* (2019, Mary Pipher says, "Long-term couples are like foxes in a den who keep each other warm and safe" (p. 194). I could not agree more. In our early years of dating, one of the many things that attracted me about Simon was his hands. They're strong and make me feel safe. They might have become that way from his years of working as a farmer's son and in the rose fields; then, too, his hands are like his father's, so surely genetics came into play there also.

I go into my closet, and, instead of grabbing yet another pair of jeans—my uniform for the quarantine of the previous year—I decide to wear a dress and two-inch heels. For the first time in nearly a year, I've decided to sit at my vanity and apply makeup. During a pandemic, a visit to the doctor can be cause for a dress-up celebration, even if the visit is a cancer checkup.

My first cancer diagnosis of breast cancer had occurred in 2001. It was the biggest shock of my adult life. Not only was there no history of cancer in my family that I knew of, I thought I'd done everything right in terms of exercising and eating well. Unfortunately, at the age of forty-seven, I had to undergo a mastectomy and reconstructive surgery a month after my daughter was released from rehab and just before the horrific events of 9/11.

Although living in Florida, I'd flown to Los Angeles to meet a world-renowned surgeon who specialized in my type of cancer, DCIS, a visit that prompted Simon's and my future relocation to the West Coast. My recovery went smoothly and I moved on, confident that cancer was behind me.

But life had other plans. At my five-year checkup in 2006, my then oncologist discovered an excessive amount of protein in my blood. Further investigation, including a bone-marrow biopsy, suggested I had multiple myeloma that supposedly wasn't connected to my earlier breast-cancer diagnosis. I was glad the condition did not yet require treatment, but it did require close monitoring with frequent blood tests by a hematologist oncologist. Most of the literature said that this type of cancer was a death sentence, but I refused to believe it. I did everything I could, including having a team of healers who worked hard to keep me healthy; and until now, seventeen years later, I've not needed treatment.

Simon sits at the kitchen table enjoying a cup of espresso. I walk past him and open a cabinet drawer stuffed with different colored masks, both patterned and solid. On the bottom of the pile are KN95 masks—the top-rated ones approved by the FDA—which are either black or white. I pick a mask with a floral pattern that matches my dress but then decide to listen to my oncologist and don a white KN95 one. Before leaving my closet, I glance in the mirror. These masks are so ugly, I think to myself. I look at my profile, and, like a hummingbird's, it looks as if I have a big beak. I feel like coloring the mask to match the hues of a hummingbird but decide to leave that for my grand-daughter on another day.

I fill my water bottle and get ready for the hour-long drive to my oncologist's office. I'm nervous, not only about meeting him but about being out in public. He's already reviewed the results of my latest blood work, which we briefly discussed on the phone. He told me that, over the past year, my multiple myeloma markers have been getting worse, and he suggested I begin treatment—chemotherapy. The amount and type of treatment varies with each person. Since 2006 when I was diagnosed, the treatment protocol has changed. There has been a lot of research resulting in

new available treatments. It used to be that patients would
have to have treatment from the time of diagnosis for the
rest of their lives. Now some need treatment for two years,
and then they go into remission. Each case is
individualized. As a former nurse, I am terrified by the idea
of chemotherapy, especially since I currently have no
apparent physical symptoms. It terrifies me because I've
seen so many people have such bad reactions to chemo. At
times it seemed that the chemo killed them before the
actual cancer did. Also, it bothered me that chemo also kills
the body's good cells.

"We're going to be late," yells Simon, a former CEO of
a tech company who always likes to be on time.

"It's fine," I say. "I'm almost ready." I pause and look
back at him. He smiles and gets up from the counter. I
leave the kitchen and step into my office. I look at the five-
by-seven, black-and-white photo of my grandmother that
has sat on my desk for nearly three decades. I believe it is
one of her modeling photos from when she lived in Vienna
before emigrating to the United States. Her dark-brown
hair was in a pageboy cut just below her ears and parted
down the middle. Her thin, painted eyebrows framed her
penetrating eyes. She wore dramatic, noir-red lipstick
applied in the shape of cupid's bow on her upper lip
outside her natural lip line.

The photograph was from the 1920s; even though she
was in her early twenties, like so many people in photos of
those times, she looks much older. Her dark-brown eyes
are wise, but, more importantly, they're all-knowing. I stop
and stare into them and ask her what she thinks of my
impending oncological visit. I ask for her thoughts about
me beginning treatment after so many years of being in
remission. There's some hesitation in her answer, as if she's
allowing space.

My grandmother, the seer, looks deeper and deeper into
my soul, and I suddenly feel a physical shift inside me.

Comfort rushes through me as she asks me what I think. When she was alive, she always told me to follow my heart; she said that our brains can fool us. Now, she asks me what messages my heart is sending and suggests that if my heart is unable to answer, I should direct my attention to my gut, or my solar plexus.

Without hesitation, I shake my head no.

"I'm not ready for chemo, Grandma."

Well, that's your answer, dear one.

"So, does that mean I don't do what my oncologist says?"

You're not ready. You'll know when you're ready, and now isn't the time. You'll be okay.

And then, with her eyes, she sends me on my way. Before I exit my office, I glance at my three pointy quartz crystals sitting in the corner of my light-wood writing desk beside the big computer monitor. The sunlight comes in from my office door, beyond which outside there's a fountain amidst my pots of red flowers where the hummingbird visits. My crystals shimmer from the light, resembling the colors of the hummingbird.

Simon calls again from the garage.

"Coming," I say.

I sit quietly in the car's passenger seat. I don't feel like talking, plus I don't know what to say. Simon is a scientist who insists that he would definitely begin treatment before symptoms emerge. I've always believed that medicine is an art more than a science, which is why we often look for physicians whose philosophies are aligned with our own. Either way, it's tough being a patient.

I look at Simon, who's already put on his seatbelt, placed his water bottle in the holder, and proceeded down the driveway to the street. We stop at the stop sign. I glance at him again, wanting to catch his eyes, window into his soul. He glances at me with a knowing smile—both of us realizing that this will be a tough day of decisions. When we were raising our three kids, now in their thirties, we sometimes had differing opinions but always found a compromise that worked for both of us. What would be the compromise regarding my treatment? It's my body, and I need to listen to its messages—and, of course, the messages relayed to me by my grandmother.

When Simon was CEO of his tech company and ready to hire an important employee, he'd call me into his office to ask my opinion about the person. He knew I had a good sense of people. Like my grandmother's, my radar is strong. Simon uses his head more than his heart. That's fine. We're all different, and that's the beauty of the universe.

We move beyond the stop sign onto the quiet suburban street. There are no other cars around. As usual, he has his left hand on the steering wheel and his right hand in his lap. I reach over and put my hand on top of his and give it a light squeeze. With a slight smile, he squeezes back and looks at me with a loving wink. He knows that I would like to hold off on treatment as long as possible. He respects my wishes and I am grateful.

~ ~ ~

I've heard that children are born with strong intuitive instincts and that at ages three to five a child is fully open and naturally intuitive. World-renowned psychic Sonia Choquette says in her book, *The Wise Child* (1999), that children experience spontaneous intuitive messages more readily than do adults, and it's important that parents listen to them. In fact, many in spiritual circles believe that young children are more intuitive and open to the otherworld because they are the most recent arrivals to Earth. Having intuition helps us observe and detect other people's behavior so that we can respond accordingly and appropriately. Those who have experienced early-childhood trauma tend to be even more intuitive because they need to be aware of everything happening in the world around them to stay safe.

Unfortunately, many times children aren't encouraged to follow their intuition, and, over time, many lose this innate sense. Encouraging the development of intuitive powers means allowing the child a lot of time for imaginary and solitary play. As an only child with very few after-school activities, especially before the age of ten, I had plenty of time to develop my intuitive powers. Intuition is also based on our experiences—what we've inherited from our ancestors as well as the emotions we encounter now in various situations. When we lose our intuitive instinct, rational thought takes over.

Intuition works more quickly than rational thought. Decisions made with rational thinking usually take longer because we need to evaluate various scenarios before making a decision. Most often intuition and rationality work together, but some individuals lean more in one direction than another.

I believe my grandmother and I survived the challenges of our childhoods and dealing with mothers who didn't cherish us by relying on and honing our instincts. I also believe that we all tend to trust our instincts more and more as we age. I noticed this during the recent years of uncertainty around the time of the coronavirus pandemic. As a result of the mixed messages we received from authorities and the universe-at-large about the disease, its course of infection, and vaccination programs, we all had more questions than answers. With scant concrete knowledge, facts, and experiences to pull from, much of our survival depended on our ability to tap into our inner wisdom. This wisdom or instinct is like a hunch we get about a person or a situation. It's a gut feeling that is sometimes called *clairsentience*—or "clear sensation," referring to an energy that is felt in our body in response to our environment, whether it comes from people, situations, places, or other realms. Children might have a difficult time explaining this feeling. They might simply say they don't feel well; they have a tummy ache or backache. Or they become tired or nervous. Personally, I just remember having this deeper knowing when things felt a little weird around me.

When we focus on listening to our inner voice, we become more empathetic and hypersensitive. I believe this is what saved Grandma during her turbulent, wartime childhood and being unwanted and then orphaned. It wasn't until I read her journal, which I will share excerpts from later, that I realized how traumatized she was by her difficult childhood. On a personal level, my inner voice is what enabled me to survive life being born to a mother who told her husband that she preferred a parakeet instead of a child. All this has given me fodder for so many stories to tell.

Writing and telling our own stories and sharing with others help us gain perspective on our experiences and navigate our own journey. Stories also unite us and can resonate at both personal and universal levels. That's one of the many reasons why people love reading and hearing them.

While I love my writing studio, it's often inspiring to write in different locations, whether it's a local coffee shop, bookstore, park, or faraway place. A few times, I have ventured off to Maui for a personal writer's retreat and had magical experiences.

On one visit, I met with a shaman who told me she thought I had been Hawaiian in a past life. This confirmed my love for Hawaiian culture. The same shaman—a tall, short-haired, fifty-something-year-old who had a smile for whoever crossed her path—said she wanted to take me to Iao Valley in West Maui. This valley is a peaceful and powerful four-thousand-acre piece of land comprising a ten-mile-long park. She picked me up in her Jeep from my hotel. We drove for about an hour through the gorgeous upcountry. When we arrived at the park, it felt as if I'd landed in a familiar, yet unnamed, magical forest. I was soon to find out why I felt so connected to the place.

After parking in the large and empty parking lot at the top of the mountain, we walked through the dense rainforest down a small hill with a stream just below.

She stopped and said, "You know, your great-grand-father had an herb farm here!"

"Really!" I responded, dying to hear more about how that was. Unfortunately, I never took the time to confirm whether I did have ancestors in that area. Maybe sometime in the future I will decide to do so.

When we finally arrived at the stream at the bottom of a small incline laden with ground cover and stones large enough to sit on, I had an unforgettable, transformative moment. I began crying like a baby. On our walk to this spot, the shaman had collected some palm leaves. At the stream, she handed them to me and told me to plant them in the water to honor my ancestors.

"Your ancestors are embracing you, and they're still with you in your heart. They said they hope you feel it."

I'd read in Dr. Foor's *Ancestral Medicine* that ancestors who embodied kindness and integrity during their lifetime can be a source of inspiration and motivation for those of us who are still living. In the same vein, they can also work to guide, uplift, and protect us. It was fascinating to me that I felt so peaceful in that moment and as if I'd come home. I became emotional and touched at a level I'd never felt before.

With tears still dripping down my face, I told the shaman that I *did* feel my ancestors and that her words really resonated with me. We spent about an hour near the stream sitting on separate rocks about twenty feet apart, watching the water flow. She suggested I pull my journal out from my backpack and write. In the past, my breast surgeon had given me a similar instruction. He had known I was a writer and was struggling post-op.

"I want you to write your story. It will help others," he told me. He was so right, as years later my book *Healing with Words: A Writer's Cancer Journey* was published.

Right there on that rock, I began writing and could not stop. The words written with my purple gel pen became a little blurred from the tears that fell onto the page. The shaman sat on her rock daydreaming and looking down at the stream. I was grateful for how she intuited that I needed time and space to be alone with my ancestors. I wrote nonstop for about an hour. On the left side of the page, I wrote letters to my ancestors; on the right side, I wrote about what I was feeling at that time.

In my letters, I thanked them for all they had taught me and were continuing to teach me. I already knew that, if we want, we can connect with our ancestors. At that time, I felt as if I were connecting with my father's relatives because the shaman said they were singing songs, and I recalled my father telling me that his family had loved singing songs on Friday evenings. I spoke to them, saying that I wished them well. I thought of my breast-cancer experience and the BRCA gene that is more prevalent in those of Jewish Ashkenazi descent. I tested for this gene mutation and do not have it; but since I have two daughters, I wonder if there's a chance they are carriers. They are approaching forty and will soon get tested. My mother, now at ninety-three, was diagnosed with metastatic breast cancer but was never tested for the gene.

When the shaman saw me stop writing and stare at the water, she tiptoed over and whispered into my right ear, "Whenever you're ready to walk, let me know."

For the rest of the day, we walked and told stories. We cried and laughed, and when I left the forest, I had a deep sense that I was leaving my real home. As we were driving away, we stopped at a farm stand that sold fruit and freshly baked bread. The friendly farmer behind the long table with local fruits smiled as the shaman got out of her truck. He said something friendly in Hawaiian. Then, he smiled at me with a knowing smile. For a moment, I felt as if she'd brought many others there and that I was just part of a bigger picture and not as special as I had thought I was. But when I thought more deeply, I wanted to believe that his eyes were telling me I was blessed to be with this amazing woman. Our subconscious brings us all sorts of messages. The entire day was a mystical experience.

During that trip in Maui, I spent a few full days alone with the shaman. At the end of each day, that tall, robust, and jovial woman full of positive energy hugged me good-bye and said, "Let's meet again tomorrow to talk story." I believe the reason I love Hawaii so much is its people's wonderful energy and the importance of story in their culture. There's something heartwarming about connecting and passing time together chitchatting and rekindling memories. Ancient Hawaiians expressed themselves through storytelling, which is known as the tradition of *moʻolelo*. This is basically the telling of stories transferred orally from one generation to the next. Moʻolelo is also an opportunity for people to channel their ancestors. According to Foor in *Ancestral Medicine* (2017), "We are bonded with the ancestors as life to death, light to shadow. The choice is not whether or not to be in relationship with them, but whether or not these relationships will be conscious or reciprocal" (p. 57).

The process is similar to what I've been doing with Grandma through the hummingbird as a messenger. There are other ways as well in which the departed might visit us. When I've discussed connecting with our ancestors in my writing workshops, some of my students have said that, if they pay attention, they get messages in all kinds of forms—from butterflies, wild animals, rainbows, and found feathers or coins to pictures, slogans, billboards, a certain piece of music, a particular numerical sequence, or electrical interferences such flashing lights or a cell phone ringing.

While I've experienced some of these occurrences during the course of my life, for me, there's something even more powerful when a hummingbird visits. I feel a renewed sense of hope and ability to see life's larger picture. These creatures also have a calming influence on me, telling me that everything happens for a reason and that everything will be okay.

Having hope is so important, especially when dealing with challenging times of all sorts, including tragedy, illness, the possibility of death, or even living through a pandemic. The stories of loved ones can help us when we listen to them. My parents were both immigrants and had so many stories to share, but also, much has been transferred down to me by the ancestral line.

Reflections / Writing Prompts

1. Discuss a memorable experience during the coronavirus pandemic.

2. Discuss a time when you felt your intuition was strong.

3. Have you ever connected with an ancestor? Describe what happened.

4. Discuss a health challenge you or your loved ones have experienced.

5. Describe an experience in which you or another child you knew was intuitive. You might also choose to write about an intuitive child you know now.

7   My Journaling Practice

We write to taste life twice, in the moment, and in the retrospection . . . We write to be able to transcend our life, to reach beyond it. We write to teach ourselves to speak with others, to record the journey into the labyrinth.

~ Anaïs Nin

The early childhood trauma of finding my grandmother dead greatly contributed to my future career as a writer. From an early age, I journaled every day as a way to cope with life's challenges. Now this is called either therapeutic writing or writing for healing. Years ago, it wasn't advocated as much as it is today. Writing brings meaning and solace, and, at the same time, relief, which fosters a heightened state of self-awareness. During my own journaling practice, I realized that I didn't have the chance to say goodbye to either of my grandparents. As a result, I was unable to process either loss adequately, reinforcing my overpowering fear of abandonment.

It might be that I carry a writing gene from my ancestors. My grandmother journaled and my mother journaled. In fact, I now call journaling my spiritual practice. Before I could drive, I'd journal in my walk-in closet or in the backyard. When I received my driver's license, I loved to sit in bookstores or cafés and make up stories about the people around me. I'd imagine what they did when they weren't there. I imagined their partners, their children, their careers, and what they did in their spare time. Once in a while, someone would see me writing in my journal and stop to ask me what I was doing. Telling them I was writing a story sometimes inspired them to share their story with me.

I've always been told that I'm easy to talk with. I guess I have a warm, inviting, and non-threatening demeanor. When my middle daughter lived in Brooklyn, we used to visit her every few months and took taxis to get around town. I was that woman who climbed into the back seat of the cab and the driver—without being solicited—would tell her their entire life story. Sometimes the stories were fascinating, but, more often than not, it was just a lonely taxi driver who wanted someone to talk to. For the most part, I didn't mind hearing other people's stories. For one thing, they reminded me of how much I wish I could have heard more of my grandmother's stories. For another, they provided fodder for my own storytelling and life as a writer.

Thanks to my grandmother and perhaps all my ancestors, during all my life's journeys I've used writing to help me heal from losses and illnesses. Over the past nearly seven decades, I've lost many loved ones—including, unfortunately, six to suicide. These were friends and family members who were dear to me, and none of the deaths were related.

In addition to my own healing, my passion has also been to teach others to use writing as a way of healing. I have suggested numerous methods to my workshop participants, but one of my students' favorites is to write a letter to a deceased loved one. The healing part of this exercise is obviously in the writing, rather than in the reading of the letter by the recipient. This letter-writing prompt is particularly useful if there are unresolved issues with the deceased or if the death was sudden. Writing gives us a chance to come to terms with losing someone. It also provides an opportunity or outlet to say what we might not have been able to say to the person when they were alive.

I am reminded of using this prompt at a workshop I facilitated years ago at a funeral home in Northern California. All the participants had lost a loved one within the previous year. It was interesting that none of the thirty participants needed to contemplate what they wanted to write. They knew exactly what had to be said. A few of the participants shared their letters with the group. One woman wrote to her dead son and apologized for the drunk driver who had killed him as he was walking across the street. Another woman pointed to the hill behind the funeral home and said as tears poured down her face, "My son is buried there. I want to put this letter on his headstone." While many of the participants wanted to keep their letters, there was a portable fire pit for those who wanted the option to burn theirs. Many cathartic tears were shed as a result of this writing experience.

While the participants were writing, I decided also to write a letter to my grandmother, something I'd done every year on the anniversary of her passing. Until I was ten years old, I'd never lost a loved one other than a goldfish dying in my fish tank or a plant withering in the living room. After Grandma died, my journal became my new companion—to help me process my losses.

As time went on, I realized how much writing nurtured me. I understood how healing and transformative the journaling practice was. And now, nearly sixty years later, I still keep a journal. My journals have become my best friends and confidantes. In them, I jot down my thoughts, passions, and dreams.

As mentioned earlier, my breast surgeon inspired me to keep a journal of my experience. During my recovery from breast-cancer surgery, I slowed down and spent time in deep contemplation and wonder. I thought about the question that, if life were to end for me tomorrow, what regrets would I have about how I had lived my life? It wasn't long afterward that I realized a big dream of mine was to go to graduate school to get an MFA in writing. I realized that dream and, as I have said, crafted my first memoir, *Regina's Closet*, from my thesis topic.

It was about that time that I stumbled upon the journals of Anaïs Nin, who's become one of my muses and favorite writers. I devoured her seven volumes of journals, which she began, as I had, as a preadolescent. Our lives have had a number of parallels, mainly in that we both began journaling as a result of a loss in our lives, and we both began our journaling passion by writing a letter to our beloved. In her situation, she began her journal (which she called a *diary*) with a letter to her father after he had left the family for a younger woman. When reading Nin's published journals, I was struck by her candor and the simplicity of her words. I wanted to emulate her writing style. I felt a magical connection with her. While reading her journals, I also began to document her wise quotations, sentiments, and reflections about life, love, writing, and loss, among other universal topics that resonated with me.

Reading Nin's work inspired my own writing, and, years later, I learned that my writing students were inspired by my story and memoirs to write their own. I delight in life's synchronicities. While I love to write, sharing my writing passion with others brings me unexpected pleasure. As I believe most passions do, my passion for teaching began early in life—in my case during my school years when I held journaling classes in my backyard.

That joy of that initial teaching experience remained with me for many years. After college, I began facilitating workshops at writing conferences and online. Many of those who attend my writing workshops are experiencing a life transition or are at a crossroads and are unsure of what they want to do. One of the first prompts I give partici-pants is to write about an important memory from their childhood. Many participants choose to write about life-changing events. My second favorite writing prompt is to ask the group to write about what they liked doing as a child. For the third prompt, I ask them to write about what brought them joy as a child and how they could bring that joy back into their life. Frequently, our childhood passions are connected to our professional callings as adults. Certainly, this was the case for me.

My mother didn't realize how buying me that Khalil Gibran journal when Grandma died led to my lifelong passion for writing. Further down the road, I journaled to help navigate challenging times such as adolescence, bed rest for all three of my pregnancies, the trials and tribulations of raising three kids, the loss of my father, the loss of friends, and my two cancer journeys. Many of my journal entries have become seeds for both small and large writing projects. For example, the journal of my first pregnancy became the impetus for a self-help book for other women who were also dealing with difficult pregnancies.

When I sit down to write, higher creative forces speak to me, and, sometimes while writing, I enter a trancelike state—I transcend universes where the deepest of creative forces are at play. I'm a poet and a memoirist, and, for each project I've worked on, there's been a different muse who guides me. Sometimes the muse is a real person, and, at other times, it's an imaginary spirit. I've had many muses during my writing life, all helping to ignite and keep my writing flame burning.

My mother was my first and longest-lived muse. Through her complicated and eccentric life, she provided me with endless stories and inspiration. Perhaps my disappointment with her as a mother sparked my need to create. When she was unavailable to me, I turned to writing. Perhaps in a sense or subconsciously, she freed the writer within me.

To be a good writer, it is important to be an avid reader. My mother did give me another important gift. Twice a month, she drove me to our local public library in Queens, one of the boroughs of New York City. When we entered through the glass doors, the librarian behind the counter smiled and said hello as I flashed her my library card. After spending an hour roaming the children's section, I'd arrive at the checkout counter with a stack of books balanced so high in my arms that it would reach up to my chin. I was excited to check them out by myself and then to be able to keep them for two weeks before returning them for someone else to enjoy. My favorite books were biographies and poetry, and that hasn't changed this many years later.

From an early age, I have always been complimented by teachers on my writing. My penmanship was okay, but what they were really speaking about was my storytelling talent. As I tell my students, to be a good writer, you need to be a good reader, as I have been since childhood. Children's passions are reinforced by the adults in their lives, so all the compliments I received encouraged me to write more and more often. Thus, the creative spark was inspired and present almost from the start.

In my early fifties, after being diagnosed with multiple myeloma, I returned to school for my doctorate in transpersonal psychology. Because of my love for writing, the program went smoothly for me. Those who struggled with writing had a more difficult time. In addition, I learned that those who are deeply passionate about something have an urgent need to make a change in the world or to serve humanity. They become possessed by their passion and are in love with their art. As Nin (1976) says, "When I don't write, I feel my world shrinking. I feel I am in a prison. I feel I lose my fire and my color. It should be a necessity, as the sea needs to heave, and I call it breathing" (p. 150).

The more I wrote, the more I realized it was my calling. There are different terms to explain the idea of one's calling in life. The Romans called it *genius*, the Greeks called it *daimon,* and the Christians call it the *guardian angel.* Psychologist James Hillman used a variety of words to describe one's calling, such as *fate, character, image, soul,* and *destiny,* depending upon the context.

When you have this type of profound passion, you're led to feelings of *bliss,* which may be defined as a natural direction to take to maximize your sense of fulfillment. It can also be viewed as feeling really, really good. Most often we feel bliss in our minds, but we can also feel it in our bodies as a happy and floaty feeling. Mythologist Joseph Campbell coined the phrase "follow your bliss," which is another way of saying to follow your heart or listen to your authentic inner voice.

To find your bliss or your calling, it's important to invite into your life people, things, and experiences that will bring out your full potential. Once you open your eyes and are aware of your bliss, opportunities start to come your way. For years, I've known that my bliss revolves around writing. Whenever people have asked me when I felt my best, I have always responded by saying, "When I'm writing." This is true whether I'm crafting poems, blogs, essays, or books.

On occasion and for inspiration, I reread my old journals, which are tucked away in boxes in my office closet. I'm so glad that I've dated them all so I can see how my feelings and perspectives have changed over the years. Sometimes my entries offer nuggets of information or thoughts to spark a new story, article, or poem. On the other hand, rereading Grandma's journal provided different offerings. They were empowering to reread during different stages in my life. Her words taught me essential lessons and gave me the strength to navigate life's challenges.

Reflections / Writing Prompts

1. Have you ever engaged in a regular journaling practice? If so, how did it go for you?

2. What writer or poet has inspired you?

3. Discuss a creative outlet that brings you joy.

4. Discuss your strongest subjects in school and how they have translated into your adult profession(s).

5. What brought you bliss as a child? What brings you bliss as an adult?

8 Finding Grandma's Journal

Our most treasured family heirlooms are our sweet memories.
The past is not dead. It is not even past.

~ William Faulkner

Two months before my forty-third birthday, my mother, who'd been widowed for more than a decade, came for a weekend visit to our home north of Montreal. When she visited from New York, she always brought with her a nostalgic item that had belonged to my father or one of my grandparents. Because my mother lived in the past, she frequently spoke about the way things used to be. She had difficulty keeping up with the changing times. She refused to learn how to use a computer, so she was asked to resign from her job as a medical receptionist in the hospital where she'd worked for twenty-five years. By that time, she was seventy-five years old.

Mother was the opposite of a hoarder. With her own sense of discretion, she tossed away anything that didn't personally serve her. She usually did this without asking anybody in the household if they wanted any of such items. For example, in 1976, when I moved out of the house to go to college, I was devastated when I learned that Mother had thrown away all my childhood journals, which were stored in a big plastic box in my closet.

Although she never spoke about why she did not like accumulating things, she did express an opinion about clothes: she believed that if you hadn't worn something in a year, chances are you'd never wear it, and therefore it was time to "get rid of it."

What is interesting is that this belief wasn't at all about being tidy. She was also very sloppy. Her bedroom often had clothes everywhere on the floor and slung over chairs and the corners of doors. Like many of her actions, this habit was inconsistent and confusing.

As an adult, I learned that clutter can be depressing for some people because it has a tendency to block energy flow. I don't think my mother consciously knew this, although subconsciously she might have known that clutter was not good for her. Like her, I also don't like clutter; however, when I declutter, I do so with discretion. Not everything is worthy of being tossed away forever. And, as a rule, I don't toss things in the garbage; I give them away to those in need, usually local organizations.

Because Mother did not like keeping things, when I was growing up I sometimes wondered when she would toss my father and me out. There were times when she made us both feel unwanted. But my father and I would make the most of our situation and do something together such as go to dinner, the car wash, or ice skating.

Before dinner on the night of my mother's arrival in Montreal, without saying anything or acknowledging their presence, she peeked into the playroom off the kitchen where my three kids were playing. She had never much liked children, nor did she know how to connect with them. I suppose that's why she left my care to my grandmother.

She came into the kitchen and lifted her small, blue suitcase onto one of the six contemporary, black-leather chairs at the table. She pulled something out and yelled to no one in particular, "Here, I brought this for you."

I stood at the counter, my back to her with my hands submerged in a bowl of chopped meat. I suspected she was speaking to me, so I turned around as she flung a plastic sheath filled with papers across the glass table.

"This is your grandmother's," she said.

What she'd tossed so unceremoniously was Grandma's journal. It wasn't a bound book or a notebook but fifty pages of single-spaced, typed pages laden with strikeovers, awkward syntax, and numerous grammatical errors. I washed my hands, walked over to the table, and collected the pages. As I flipped through them, a sudden strong memory overtook me: the day my grandmother taught me how to type on her Remington typewriter when I was eight years old. I wondered if it had been the same typewriter that she'd used to type this journal.

"Have a seat on this chair," Grandma had said, pointing to her vanity chair. "I'm going to teach you how to type. This is a handy skill for a girl to have. Plus, you never know what kind of stories you'll want to tell one day."

With her blonde hair in bouffant style and her bright red lipstick framing the space between her two front teeth, she stood behind me, smiling radiantly in the mirror. She took my right hand and positioned it on the second row of keys from the bottom, carefully placing one finger on each letter. With my left hand, she repeated the same gesture.

"This is the position your fingers should be in. When you become a good typist, you won't even have to look at the letters while you're typing. Okay, dear, let's see if we can type your name."

With my left middle finger, she had me press on the *D*. Then we moved to the right middle finger and moved up a row to type an *I*. Then my pinky pressed the *A*, and then something tricky needed to happen: I had to move my right index finger down to the bottom row to type an *N*. My left pinky typed an *A* again. After each letter, I glanced at the paper to see the impression my efforts were making. After reaching the last *A* in my name, I proudly looked up at my grandmother's face in the mirror.

"You see, you did it!" she said, squeezing my shoulders. "Like anything in life, the more you practice, the better you'll become. You must work hard to get results. You'll learn that soon enough, my love."

That typing lesson reflected the essence of the relationship between my beloved grandmother and me. She loved teaching me and honored the person I would become.

Now, in my kitchen, I carefully removed her journal pages from their sheath and noticed that they were yellowing, fragile to the touch, and that some of the edges were slightly torn. I was afraid to hold them or to put them down—terrified that all those cherished memories could get lost or ruined. What if someone spilled coffee on them?

"How long have you had this? How come you're so casual about giving it to me?" I asked my mother.

"I wasn't sure if you'd be interested."

"*What*? Are you crazy? How could I not be interested? You know I'm a writer and an ardent reader, and these are the words of the only grandmother I ever knew, plus she was my primary caretaker!"

"I found them when I was going through some papers in her closet," she said, walking toward the family room to sit on the sofa, completely oblivious to my eight-year-old son, assembling a Lego house on the shaggy, beige rug.

I rushed through dinner preparations and feeding my family and asked my husband to do the dishes so I could dive into reading Grandma's journal. It took only a few moments for me to be immersed in her story, mesmerized by her childhood pain and swept away by her sense of rhetoric. Her voice lifted off the page. I wanted to hug her, to take her into my arms and soothe her. Yet, at the same time, her epic story gave me strength and hope as to what a woman can endure and how someone can survive despite all odds. I thought about my own survival stories and cancer journeys when, more than ever, I had needed my grandmother's love and support. I felt that our survival stories were a thread that bound us together. I also discovered another thread: we were both born to mothers who didn't want us; nor were they capable of loving us in the way we know mothers often do.

I read every word, felt every intonation, every pain, and every rare moment of joy. It was impossible to stop reading. My eyes began burning from smudged mascara. I read, wanting to know everything about my grandma and to infuse myself with her essence. I yearned to hear her wisdom and absorb her teachings. I wanted to capture love from her story—the unconditional love that I missed so much.

Suddenly, after receiving her journal, I was reunited with her for the first time since she'd died more than thirty years earlier. It felt both eerie and exciting. Her voice once again filled the gap of the loneliness born out of being an only child and being raised by a mother with narcissistic tendencies who really did not understand me nor know how to bring out the best in me.

I learned that, even though my grandmother had three siblings, she leaned toward loneliness. Her two older brothers didn't take much interest in her, and she wasn't close with her younger sister whom she took care of after their parents died during the cholera pandemic in the early twentieth century.

When Grandma was eleven years old, the cholera pandemic struck their hometown of Galicia, which at the time was in Poland. That pandemic differed from the COVID-19 pandemic in that people had no idea why they were becoming ill. One day, Ethel, my grandmother's mother, said she wasn't feeling well, and, late that night when the children were asleep, her husband took her to the infirmary, where she was quarantined. When my grandmother woke up early in the morning and found her parents gone, she couldn't get back to sleep. She intuited that something bad had happened.

In her journal, Grandma wrote about how, at four o'clock in the morning, while her siblings were still asleep, she quietly got dressed, grabbed a flashlight, tiptoed barefoot outside, and headed to the infirmary to see if she could find her mother. On her way, all sorts of images of her mother overwhelmed her. She walked a few blocks on the empty cobblestone streets. The only sign of life was a rat rummaging in the garbage in front of the grocery store. At the end of the village was a big, open field with small and large trees scattered across it. She knew the infirmary was on the other side of the field. She trotted over the green expanse, stopping every so often to lift her foot and remove a pebble that was caught between her toes. Using the flashlight, she scanned the area, checking for any creatures.

As the sun rose over the horizon, she approached a barren building at the far edge of the field. There were no trees, only a high fence that was too high for her to jump or climb over. She wondered why an infirmary had to be fenced in, given that the people inside the building were very sick. Why would they want to leave if they weren't feeling well?

At the far corner of the building, a guard stood with his rifle poised at his side, the bayonet pointing straight into the air. He was diligently guarding the infirmary. My grandmother sensed he wouldn't allow her to go inside. She walked toward him, and he suddenly turned and walked around the corner of the building. As soon as she could no longer see him, she ran along the edge of the fence, found an opening, and quickly wiggled her way through it. She looked left and right before dashing into the long, cement building.

Gingerly, she tiptoed inside the front door, but in reality, nobody could really hear her because she was barefoot on a cold, concrete floor. There was no one standing inside the entrance. She found this strange, especially since there was a guard standing *outside* the building. As far as she could see inside, the halls were lined with rows and rows of occupied beds. There were delirious old people who rambled nonsensically. Others lay completely still and silent. She didn't know if the unmoving were dead or asleep. To her they all looked so very pale.

As she ventured farther down the cold corridor, she saw that not only were all the beds filled, but sick people were also lying on the straw-covered floor, a floor so slick with vomit that she stumbled and fell. As she lay there, a dark-haired woman lying on the floor squirmed in her direction, grabbed her arm, and hung on. My grandmother shook her off, pulled herself up onto her feet, and continued searching for her mother. In desperation, another woman yanked at Grandma's long dress and begged for water. Grandma kept walking, weaving in and out of the bodies, desperately trying not to step on them. To her horror, every face seemed to look similar to her mother's.

After searching in vain for an hour, she decided to give up. Seeing all the dead and dying people had emotionally drained her. She walked out of the infirmary and looked for the hole in the fence, but she couldn't find it. The sun was now well above the horizon. She saw the guard at the corner of the building and scrambled in the opposite direction, crouching down along the fence to camouflage herself. All of a sudden, he turned and spotted her. He waved his rifle in the air, cursing something in German, and then ran toward her. She hurried on, frantically continuing to look for the hole in the fence, which she finally found. She slipped through and ran as fast as her feet would carry her. The guard never caught her but kept yelling in a language she didn't understand.

Halfway back home, she stopped to rest and catch her breath. Completely drained of energy, she sat under a shaded tree in the middle of the field. She couldn't stop crying and praying. She leaned against the tree and stared at the infirmary. She wanted to believe her mother was still alive somewhere inside the building, but she was overcome by bleakness.

A part of her wanted to return to that terrible place and search one more time. But another part of her was actually scared to find her mother. From her apron pocket, my grandmother pulled out a handkerchief and the only photo she had of Ethel. In the grainy image, her mother sat on the porch mending socks. Her handkerchief drenched with tears, my grandmother wondered if she'd ever see her again. Overwhelmed by feelings of hopelessness, isolation, and frustration, she wished she weren't alone at such a terrifying moment in her young life.

Here is Grandma's journal entry from later that morning:

I stood up, stretched out my arms toward the heavens and glanced down at my dirty feet. In an effort to keep warm, I hugged myself. On the way back home from the infirmary, I walked along the fence toward the mortuary on the other side of the field. The building looked similar to the infirmary except it had only two windows, one on either side. As I approached the building, one part of me wanted to rush inside, yet another part of me was absolutely terrified.

There were no guards or fences outside the mortuary. The door was wide open. I entered and stood at the doorway while my eyes shifted from left to right. Corpses were lying on the floor covered in their own garments. It seemed to me that in the distance I saw my mother's black skirt lying over a body. There was a brush-like trim on the bottom hem, just like my mother's. I was sure it was her. As I began walking toward the bodies, a worker approached me, motioning for me to come to the information desk.

I staggered to the wooden desk. A nun sat stiffly behind it. I told her I was looking for my mother. She assured me that my mother was sick, but that she would eventually be fine. But, in my heart, I knew she was lying to me, and that my mother's body was somewhere in that immense room. I knew too well that there was no mother for me anymore. The nun implored me to go home. I walked slowly back through the field, feeling no sense of resolve from my morning journey. When I arrived back home, I plunked down on my bed. My family had already woken up and gone out somewhere. I had little energy to look for them or begin my day and do all my chores. Nothing mattered to me anymore.

The following day, there was a knock on the front door of my grandmother's house:

"Good morning, I'm looking for the family of Mrs. Reinharz," said a stern-looking doctor. There was a stethoscope in his jacket pocket, and he bore a solemn expression.

"Yes, I'm her eldest daughter," my grandma said.

"I'm so sorry to inform you that your mother has died. If you want to see her before she's buried with the other cholera victims, you need to come with me now. If not, you'll never see her again."

Grandma stood there, frozen and without words. How could she endure any more pain in her young life? She refused to go view her mother, and she didn't explain why in her journal. I imagine it was too overwhelming, especially in light of what she'd seen in the days prior.

Shortly thereafter, Grandma's father was also taken to the infirmary for quarantine, and he died a few hours later. Suddenly, there she was, an eleven-year-old orphan, forced to run the household with her eight-year-old sister. Nobody was there to look after the two young girls, their two older brothers having already made plans to leave for Vienna to look for new jobs and a new life. Sadly, the brothers didn't care much about what would become of their two sisters.

Over the years, I have often pulled out Grandma's journal to reread it. My intention has been to absorb her sensibilities and understand who she was and what she endured. I also wanted to understand her sense of torment and what led to her depression and subsequent suicide. I knew that certain psychological traits can be genetic. While we do have control over our lives, genetics is an important factor that can determine whether, when facing life's setbacks, we feel grateful or doomed. I thought it was critical for me to know everything I could about my grandmother's mental health, hoping it would help me navigate my own journey. Even though her story was sad, reading it grounded me and brought me closer to her. Her words empowered me. They also served as a reminder of my huge sense of loss and abandonment when she died.

Until receiving the journal, I had no idea that Grandma was a journal keeper as I am. Sometimes when we study and get to know our ancestors, we make fascinating discoveries. Perhaps journaling is in my DNA. For years, it has been my savior.

Reflections / Writing Prompts

1. Do you have an artifact or item that reminds you of an ancestor?

2. What passions have you carried with you since childhood?

3. Did a grandparent have a talent or passion that they shared with you?

4. Is there a memorable story that a parent or grandparent shared about their own childhood?

5. What were some of the challenges that your parents and/or grandparents faced?

9   Ancestral Trauma, Demons, and the Search for Meaning

What is silenced in the first generation, the second generation carries in the body.

~ Francoise Dolto

During 2020, the first full year of the coronavirus pandemic, I again pulled out my grandmother's journal. I was tempted to compare the trajectory of the cholera pandemic she lived through more than a century before the pandemic of my lifetime.

There are differences and similarities. The obvious differences are in the communications and medical realms. There was no Internet back then, so dispensing news or information was much more challenging. It sometimes took time for information to travel from one village to the next. There was also little knowledge of the importance of healthy and hygienic habits such as mask wearing, handwashing, and maintaining social distance to prevent disease transmission.

Cholera is caused by a waterborne bacterium that kills quickly. Its victims can die in as little as eight hours after contracting the disease. During Grandma's childhood, there were no water-purification systems. There were also no vaccines. The treatment for cholera was hydration and salt replenishment. Antibiotics were only discovered in the late 1920s and were used to treat cholera only in later pandemics, not in the cholera scourge of my grandmother's time.

Grandma often quoted the truism that history repeats itself. I suspect she was mainly referring to the events of world history, but history within the family unit also repeats itself. When we tap into the characteristics and experiences of our ancestors, we are bound to learn of both positive and negative attributes that are passed down through the bloodlines or DNA.

Ancestral or intergenerational healing comes into play when we try to understand, cope with, and accept the wounds of our ancestors and try not to have them affect our lives.

Creating healthy connections with our ancestors is an important key. Dr. Rachel Yehuda, a professor of psychiatry and neuroscience and a pioneer in understanding cross-generational trauma, was interviewed by Krista Tippett on one of my favorite podcasts, *On Being* (2017). They discussed the new field of epigenetics, which "sees that genes can be turned on and off and expressed differently with changes in environment and behavior." That is, trauma and resilience "can transmit biologically, beyond cataclysmic events, to the next generation."

It's important to know the stories of our ancestors and that they are also *our* stories; but at the same time, they're not *really* our stories. We have to create our own narrative of our own life, without holding on to all our ancestors' grief and tribulations. A healthier way is to send previous generations love and compassion while living our own lives. It is all very bittersweet.

I cannot deny the fact that depression is inherited, and I've always been interested in how my grandmother dealt with the demons associated with it. While my childhood demons weren't as horrific as hers, as each of us heads into adulthood, we're left with different types of scars, and I don't want to succumb to the same fate she did.

In her book *Ordinary Genius* (2009), poet Kim Addonizio says that everyone has demons. Sometimes they're apparent to others and sometimes they are hidden. On the outside, people see me as a bright and positive person, but, on occasion, I do battle with depression. Those who have done work with ancestral healing have said that children and grandchildren of Holocaust survivors are more prone to depression and anxiety than most people. Helen Epstein speaks about this in her book *Children of The Holocaust* (1988). There are many possible causes, both physiological and psychological. On a personal level, sometimes I'm able to cope by engaging in my spiritual practices of daily meditation, journaling, and acupuncture, while at other times I need to reach out for medicinal interventions.

I'm fascinated by the psychological factors that result in depression because I believe it is what contributed to my grandmother's demise. Depression is often a precursor to suicide. Unmet needs coupled with hopelessness feeds depression. While she did not go through the Holocaust, she did survive trauma during World War I in Poland. Did she lose hope because of what she'd been through? Or did she lose hope because of how her present-moment life was unfolding?

In Viktor Frankl's classic book, *Man's Search for Meaning* (2006), he writes about how being hopeful aided his ultimate survival in the concentration camps. He also writes about the importance of having a life purpose. Even though his philosophy emerged from his time in the camps, it has wide applications. To survive the most challenging times, one must have a life purpose. Having a life purpose means liberating our potential with the goal of bettering ourselves. It's also about feeling a sense of interconnectedness with others, mindfulness practice, compassion, and being more conscious of our actions.

A few years after my grandmother died, I heard my mother tell her friend that Grandma took her life because I was becoming more independent and no longer needed her. It didn't really bother me at the time, but, as the years moved along, I realized that the true reason for her depression and ultimate demise was that the trauma of her childhood lived on in her body and finally became unbearable. It is also true, however, that until I was nine or so, her life revolved around being my caretaker—walking me to school, preparing my meals, and helping me with my homework. My needs gave her life a sense of purpose. When I began to prepare my own lunches and wanted to walk to school by myself, she no longer felt needed.

The importance of being needed can't be overemphasized, and I see this in my own life as a grandmother. Even though I am still involved with my writing practice and publishing, the mere act of babysitting for a few hours a week brings me so much pleasure and provides a deep sense of life purpose. I also contemplate my responsibility as an elder and the important teachings that my grandchildren glean from my life experiences. If they don't learn about their past from me, who will they learn it from?

The weekend before my grandmother's suicide, my parents and I went on a family weekend holiday to Bermuda, which was a popular travel destination back in the 1960s. It was the first time we hadn't invited Grandma to join us on a family trip. Perhaps that was what led her to her depression and ultimate suicide. She saw her life purpose coming to an end. While my mother never voiced it to me, I wonder if she subconsciously felt responsible for Grandma's suicide, since she was the one who decided not to invite her on our holiday.

As a mother of three and a grandmother of six, I clearly understand the importance of being needed. Being needed gives us a sense of significance, whether it's on a personal, community, or universal level.

When each of my daughters had their first child, they lived in states on the other side of the country. One of my daughters asked me to come help, while the other said she was fine and didn't need me. My heart was warmed to hear that I was needed by one but somewhat hurt by the other who said I wasn't needed. In all honesty, I wasn't thinking about what her predicament was; I was just thinking of my need to help and be a part of her life. Even as a writer with a busy freelance career, I have always put my family's needs first. It gives me a deep sense of pleasure to be called upon to help. I love to be needed.

It's important to know what brings us joy and to express it to our loved ones. During the first year of the COVID-19 pandemic, I couldn't as easily hop onto an airplane and visit my daughter in Florida, but I felt a deep need to be part of my grandchildren's lives. So, I sent gifts and used FaceTime as much as possible. Thankfully, my son did move nearby with his wife when she was expecting their first child, and I felt the void of being needed would be filled. But then I saw that I wasn't needed after all because my daughter-in-law's mother was always present, so I decided to volunteer at a vaccination clinic. For me, offering to help others is a way to stay in the light and out of the darkness. It's also a way to get out of my own head when battling depression and loneliness.

Today in our culture, there's less shame in admitting we're depressed. Many people openly admit that they see a therapist for regular chats or to guide them through life's tribulations. In the 1960s, when my grandmother was struggling with depression, she approached Dr. Robbins, our family doctor. Dr. Robbins was a cartoon character of a doctor, a classic of the times. He was overweight, wore frameless bifocals at the tip of his nose, and smoked a pipe that hung from his lips even during physical exams. His office was in part of his house but had a separate entrance. Beyond the entrance was a small vestibule with a receptionist, and from there you went right into the doctor's office, which doubled as an examination room. On one side of the room was a small examination table, lined with paper leading down to the stirrups at the end. On the other side was a rather large, leather-top desk with books stacked on each side and an ashtray full of ashes. There was a deep, pungent odor coming from the doctor's pipe. He had a jovial laugh and a bright smile with big, rosy cheeks. After he performed an exam, he'd ask the patient to sit in the chair facing his desk as he sat jotting down notes while puffing on his pipe. He tried to blow the smoke to the side, but it inevitably arrived in our faces. On the corner of his desk sat a doctor's bag, which told the viewer that he was ready for house calls.

Dr. Robbins loved women and was quite flirtatious. When I turned sixteen, he suggested I have my first gynecological exam, which, in those days, was done by the family doctor. After that first exam, he told me to sit by his desk so we could talk. He began by saying that I'd have a great sex life but never explained why. He then handed me a copy of Rollo May's *Love and Will.* Since I was still a virgin and hadn't yet had a long-term boyfriend, much of the book made no sense to me, but I kept it in a secret spot in my closet. While in graduate school, I discovered May's book *The Courage to Create,* which I loved. It served as a reminder to reread *Love and Will,* which was somewhat outdated but an interesting read, nevertheless.

When my grandmother visited Dr. Robbins only a few weeks before she died, I imagine she was well dressed and exhibited perfect posture, as if going for a modeling shoot—wearing a two-piece suit and a fur-collared coat with high heels. During that appointment, she probably sat before his desk with her legs crossed at the ankles and clutching her matching purse on her lap. I sense this because she always told me to dress nicely when I left the house, even if it was just to put out the garbage. "You never know, dear, who you can meet at the curb!"

I imagine Dr. Robbins's conversation with my grandmother went something like this:

"Hello, Regina, my dear. It's so wonderful to see you. Don't you look stunning today!"

"Thank you, Doctor."

"What brings you in? I believe you had your annual not too long ago."

"Dr. Robbins, I've been feeling *off* lately. I'm very sad and am having trouble sleeping."

"Oh, I'm sorry to hear that. It happens sometimes to women as they get older. How old are you now?"

"I'm sixty-one."

"Yes, of course. Now, why don't I give you a prescription for Valium? It will help you sleep much better. It's best to take it just as you go to bed to ensure you get a good night's sleep."

While this consultation might have helped Grandma overcome her acute issues, it didn't help her long term. She was lonely and needed somebody to talk to, but psychotherapy was not readily available. Unfortunately, that prescription for Valium was what ended up killing her.

Reading the story of my grandmother's life certainly gave me perspective and made me realize how blessed I am to be living at a time when there's no stigma associated with mental-health issues and when asking for help if you need it—whether it's for talk therapy or medication—is acceptable and, in fact, commonplace. It saddens me that she didn't have such help available to her.

~ ~ ~

I believe we're all the result of our childhoods, and many of the challenges and difficulties we face during adulthood are due to childhood-born demons. My grandmother's early days laid the foundation for a tumultuous life. When I reread her story, it feels as if she'd been doomed nearly from the start.

Grandma Regina was born in Kalush, Galicia (now western Ukraine), on June 22, 1903. Her journal, which she began after emigrating to the United States in 1930, recounted her story from the time she was eleven, starting in 1914 at the beginning of World War I:

I am a war child, and here is my story. I was born an undesired child, a girl added to two brothers. When my mother, after her delivery, was told I was a girl, she fainted. When she came to her senses, she said she would gladly kill me because of my being a girl. She said she would have pre-ferred six boys to one female, because, she argued, a female suffers too much in this world. I grew up and quickly distinguished good from bad treatment. I saw that she discriminated against me and acted as if she resented my being born—as if it were my fault. I spent a lot of time on the streets. Everyone in the community really liked me. I was amiable and beguiling and always willing to help others.

A few times each week, I would open my bedroom window and climb out to the street below. I tried being as quiet as possible because my sister, who was four years younger, slept in the same room. But she never woke up. I would then wander up the street chatting with the Ukrainian peasants and watching as they brought cows, pigs, and eggs to the local market. It was here where I learned some basic entrepreneurial skills.

I was touched by my grandmother's transparency when writing about her mother, Ethel, and how she was un-wanted and didn't feel loved. Ethel's words were harsh and certainly difficult for Regina to hear. I wish I'd had the chance to talk to her about her relationship with her mother. Maybe I could have learned something about my relationship with my own mother. Only when I became an adult did I come to grips with and begin to understand that relationship. In addition to being interested primarily in her own needs, I believe my mother has always been somewhat uncomfortable in her own skin. In some ways, I intimidated her. She was jealous of my father's love for me and my many accomplishments in life.

I believe my pursuit of the advanced degrees of a MFA and PhD was driven in part by my mother's attitude toward me. I wanted to prove to myself that I could succeed in whatever I wanted to do and that I wasn't stupid—and my mother was disappointed when I chose to write in my journals rather than do my homework or study for my exams.

The truth is that we understand and appreciate more about our primary caretakers as we mature and reflect upon our childhood with adult eyes. In my workshops, I remind the participants that voice is very important in memoir writing and that what's most fascinating to readers is the composite voice. This voice tells the story from a child's viewpoint while also viewing our experiences from an adult perspective. The truth is that children don't have the tools to acknowledge or understand the challenges facing them. They live in a day-to-day mode. Children have a lot to teach us about mindfulness practice.

From an early age, Grandma had an amazingly free spirit, and she exerted it whenever the opportunity presented itself. Like her, I have also been a spiritual seeker following a path of self-discovery. This path is a lifelong pursuit that often results from an early pivotal event or trauma. For my grandmother, the event was losing her parents at a young age; and for me, it was losing my grandmother, my beloved caretaker, at nearly the same age. Many spiritual seekers come from dysfunctional families. We tend to look for places of refuge and comfort.

Here's what poet Rainer Maria Rilke says in *Letters to a Young Poet* (1993) about the importance of being a seeker:

> Be patient toward all that is unsolved in your heart
> and try to love the questions themselves, like locked
> rooms and like locked books that are written in a
> very foreign tongue. Do not now seek the answers,
> which cannot be given you because you would not
> be able to live them. And the point is, to live every-
> thing. Live the questions now. Perhaps you will
> then gradually, without noticing it, live along some
> distant day into the answer.

I'll never know if Grandma's spirit was a result of her not sensing motherly love or if it was simply part of her inborn personality. I speculate that it was a combination of the two. Her spirit resonates with who I am. When re-reading her journal and staring at her photo on my desk, I sense her spirit at a deep level.

Because my grandmother believed she was unwanted, as a child she looked for attention and adoration from adults in her neighborhood. She reached out to those in her small village by running errands and helping people with their daily chores. Later in her life, I believe she transferred this need for attention and love to both my mother and me. By giving herself completely, in return, she received our love and appreciation.

Reflections / Writing Prompts

1. Discuss any diseases or illnesses that affected your parents and/or grandparents.

2. Do you believe that history repeats itself? If so, provide examples.

3. Is there any intergenerational healing that needs to occur within your family?

4. What are your demons and the demons of your ancestors?

5. In what way do you feel that you honor your ancestors?

10 Dealing with Childhood Scars

The power of trauma is that it has both the power to destroy and the power to transform and resurrect.

~ Peter A. Levine

Like most children who didn't receive unconditional motherly love, my grandmother was left with emotional scars that impacted her for the rest of her life. I felt terrible when I read the following section of her journal retelling an event that happened one Saturday when she was five years old:

I woke up early and wanted to surprise my mother by washing all the windows in our small house. After washing for about one hour, I accidentally broke a windowpane, and it shattered all over the kitchen floor. I was devastated, because I knew that it didn't take much for my mother to be angry at me, and this would surely upset her. She did not respond well to any change or mishap in her daily routine, plus she was very particular about her house, especially her kitchen.

I stood completely still, afraid to move. Suddenly, I heard my mother's bedroom door open and she staggered out half asleep. She came toward me standing still in the kitchen. I was petrified at what she might say or do. She was so unpredictable. Instead of asking me what I was doing or even saying thank you for washing the windows, she yelled at me and asked how I could do such a thing. I was afraid to answer, because no matter what I said, she would still be angry. She began spanking me and then sent me off to my room.

I wondered how a mother could be so cruel to a young, well-meaning daughter. In comparison, although my mother wasn't the most compassionate person, she wasn't mean in that way. But still, for most of my life, I never felt adored, cherished, or protected by her. She had a difficult time showing me love; she never gave me a compliment or bragged about me to others. This was especially difficult to endure when I saw other mothers compliment their children. The only exception has been in her later years when dementia has begun to settle in. She's become kinder and more appreciative. I suppose that is the silver lining of the onset of her mental impairment.

My students sometimes tell me that when they read my memoirs or articles about my experiences, it often triggers memories of their own. I've always found memory triggers to be interesting. So many incidents in my grandmother's journal sparked my own memories. For example, her story about breaking her mother's window triggered the following memory from my own childhood.

For my twelfth birthday, my mother gifted me with a family heirloom—a ring my grandmother had given her when Mother graduated from high school. It was a striking, yellow-gold, rectangular ring with seven diamonds and rubies diagonally positioned. The ring was oversized for my finger, so, to give it a snugger fit, my mother wrapped Scotch tape around the underside of the band.

"Just wear it for special occasions, like going out to dinner," she said.

The next week, we went to dinner to Horn & Hardart, a food-service company noted for its automats. We went there at least once a week, and my favorite meal was lamb shoulder, mashed potatoes, and corn. After placing my order with the waitress, with my pigtails swinging back and forth and wearing my favorite red plaid skirt, I slid out of the booth and scurried down the spiral staircase to wash my hands in the bathroom. My father was a clean freak and always reminded me to wash my hands before eating.

The bathroom was empty. There was a line of four white pedestal sinks with soap dispensers on the wall above. After leaving the stall, I went to the first sink near the towel machine, removed the ring and placed it beside the faucet, washed my hands, and ran back upstairs. As I sat down, my mother glanced at my hand.

"Diana, where's the ring?"

Gasping, I bolted across the black-and-white checkered linoleum floor and sped down the stairs to the bathroom. The ring was gone. The hostess and the manager searched everywhere, but the ring never turned up.

"How could you do that?" my mother reprimanded. "You should be ashamed of yourself!" She was so angry that she didn't eat her dinner that night.

Given this experience and a few similar ones, I wondered if something was wrong with me. I often felt so much shame, and yet I never understood what I did that was so terrible. I also wondered why my mother was so different from all the other mothers in my school, who didn't have jobs and waited at home after school with home-baked cookies.

I suppose that, from the outside, we looked like a normal family. When I was in elementary and middle school, all my friends thought my mother was cool because she worked in a doctor's office, rode horses on the weekend, and did yoga on the beach. While it sounded interesting to outsiders, behind closed doors, my mother was a different person. She was often sour faced and spent hours curled up on the sofa crying. I don't think she liked being part of a family unit, and in addition she mourned the loss of her mother for many years. In fact, I don't think my mother liked belonging at all. She was always more comfortable with the natural world and animals than she was with people.

She was in her late eighties when I had to sell her house and move her to a suitable assisted-living facility. I made sure to find one near a forested area where she could watch the birds. I bought a special hummingbird feeder for her window, hoping she'd begin to have visitations.

For years afterward, she was mad at me for making this decision to move her into one of those places. It was really not what I wanted for her, but I had no choice. My mother and I lived on opposite coasts. Being an only child, I had no one else to help her with me, and I could no longer manage her care by myself long distance.

I decided to find her a place the day my son called while visiting her in her suburban house in northern Long Island, where she lived alone. He was a very handsome young man—thick auburn hair, dimples, and six feet tall. Quite mature for his age and always a charmer, he was able to charm women of all ages. Once when we took a family holiday when he was thirteen, a twenty-eight-year-old hotel employee had hit on him.

The day my son called while visiting my mother in Long Island, he had been upset.

"Mom, I just drove an hour to see Evie [what my children call her]. There's a lot of snow. When I got here, I went around to the side entrance, and I saw her lying in the snow in her nightgown."

"*What?* Are you kidding me? What was she doing there?"

"She said she was putting food into the bird feeder and, on her way back to the house, she tripped on something under the snow and then couldn't get up."

I should mention that, as she aged, my mother had become grossly overweight, especially after she stopped horseback riding, and, as a result, did a lot of emotional eating.

"I don't know what would have happened to her if I hadn't made a surprise visit," my son went on. "She didn't even have the cell phone we bought her in her pocket. It was uncharged on her dining room table."

"Oh, my. That's terrifying," I said.

My son had helped her to her feet and walked her inside, placing her on her sofa. Then he went to get something from his car and noticed her rust-color Mazda parked beside his. He phoned me back.

"Mom, you should see her car. It's a mess. There are swipes on both sides and the side mirrors are both knocked off."

The description of my mother's car brought back images of her taking me to the stable every Sunday and loading up the back seat (where I sat) with buckets of manure to fertilize the vegetable garden. The memory of that odor still elicits waves of nausea.

At that time, my son was in university and had a big exam the following day. I knew he could only stay with Mom for a few hours. I immediately phoned her cleaning lady to see if she could be more available to help Mom until I could figure out a plan and get to New York. After researching the best assisted-living facilities, I chose the one I felt best suited her and then flew to New York to get her settled in. *That* was a day to remember.

Because of a series of unfortunate events leading up to that day, my mother was no longer able to ambulate and had become wheelchair bound. So, to move her, I ordered a transport service. It was a forty-five-minute drive from her house to her new home at the Long Island facility. During that trip, Mother didn't say a word. When I asked her a question, she stared out the window and pretended she didn't hear me. If I could have felt emotional temperatures, hers would have been ice cold. She completely shut down.

When we pulled up to the front of the facility, she glanced out the window and said, "I never thought I'd end up here."

It was difficult to know what to say. After a pregnant pause, I offered, "I looked for a place where there were lots of trees and birds outside your apartment window."

She didn't respond.

During the best of times, my mother was never talkative or appreciative, especially if the discussion didn't involve her. My father and I were people lovers and often felt sorry for her because she wasn't.

Her new apartment was lovely—carpeted, bright, and airy, with two windows overlooking a forested area. It was perfect for birdwatching. I unpacked her belongings, but she remained silent and refrained from looking me in the eyes.

"Mom, would you like to have tea in the café with me?"

"Okay," she said, but her countenance remained glum.

We made our way to the self-serving café, and I pushed her up to one of the tables that accommodated wheelchairs.

"Do you want tea or coffee?"

"Black coffee."

"Would you like a pastry to go with it?"

"No."

For most of her life, regardless of the situation, my mother's answers were typically abrupt and ungrateful. I sat beside her and had a passing thought that maybe this would be the last time I'd see her before returning to California.

After serving us both our beverages, I took a breath and then said, "So, Mom, this might seem like a big question, but I feel compelled to ask you. If you had the chance to live your life over again, how might you do it differently?"

She stared into the distance out the window overlooking the grass.

For the first time, I thought I had an opportunity to tap into my mother's psyche and learn things I'd not known before. Maybe she would divulge new information. Maybe I would get a thank you—something! I was excited to learn more about her and what was going on inside her head. For years, I'd caught her staring into space, looking contemplative and disappointed about something. She often seemed tormented, and nobody seemed to know her entire story. Was she guarding a big secret that she couldn't share? Did she feel the end of her life approaching now, and, if so, would that make her more open? Since she'd always been in denial of her age—writing on forms that she was five to ten years younger than she actually was—I doubted she'd acknowledge her mortality.

All of a sudden she responded. "Well, I wouldn't have gotten married, and I *certainly* wouldn't have had children!"

As an only child, I had devoted a great deal of time to her well-being, especially after my father had died many years earlier. I felt a stabbing pain in my chest. It took me a moment to process her comment and a little longer to respond. I wanted to ask her to repeat herself. Perhaps I'd heard her incorrectly. *Did she hate me that much?*

After gathering my composure, I said, "Sorry to hear you say that. Sounds like you have many regrets."

She continued to stare straight ahead, refusing to look me in the eyes. That moment truly summed up her feelings about me. What's interesting to note is that, after she had been at the facility for five years, I posed the same question, and she actually said that she had no regrets. Even though dementia had begun settling in, she seemed lucid at the time and, perhaps without admitting it to me, realized that I was the only one in the world who really cared about her. She had no friends, and my children were not inspired to visit or call because she was not very nice to them, often criticizing them or putting them down, as she had me when I was a young girl.

~ ~ ~

So, both my grandmother and I had mothers who, for no apparent reason—or a small reason—chose to be angry with us and certainly made us feel unwanted. Whether it was jealousy of the compassionate and driven women we were or something else, I'll never know; nor will I know what caused my mother to be the type of person she was. I know very little about her childhood except that she emigrated to the United States from Austria in 1939.

Regardless, I continued to respect her and honor her as the woman who gave me life. I've learned to come to terms with the fact that she is who she is. I have worked hard to accentuate the positive aspects of her personality (we all have some), such as loving animals, buying me my first journal, and taking me to the library every week. I am reminded of a comment the singer Tina Turner made in the wonderful HBO documentary about her, *Tina* (2021): "I took care of and treated my mother as if she loved me." Even though Tina had a troubled relationship with her mother, she always took care of her. In fact, when the singer became famous, she bought her mother a house. This sentiment resonates with me.

Reflections / Writing Prompts

1. Do you have a childhood story about when you felt a certain amount of shame?

2. Discuss a time when you felt a parent was not acting reasonably.

3. What recent event triggered you to think of a childhood event?

4. What was your most cherished childhood gift, and why?

5. Describe what communication was like in your family unit when you were a child.

11   Honoring Poignant Words

A lot of people have gone further than they thought they could because someone else thought they could.

~ Zig Ziglar

As a wordsmith, I understand the power of words, whether they are verbal or written. Words can soothe and heal, but they can also hurt. For this reason, my father taught me to think before I spoke. As a published writer, I've been blessed with a couple of memorable mentors who not only supported me but said things about my writing that I'll never forget. I hold those words with the deepest gratitude. The sentiments have an air of purity and honesty that we might not feel from everybody who is familiar with or reads our work. Their praise counts for something powerful in our lives that gives us the courage we need to reach even higher. The inspiration they provide is unmatched.

I rarely knew what Mother was thinking—or I was afraid to ask. As a child, I came to understand that she probably didn't care about me or my grades. She was quick to make a positive comment about how I was dressed but reluctant to compliment me on good behavior or attitudes, which, as an adult, I view to be much more important. Thus, I frequently received confusing messages from her. She was often wrapped up in her own world, and I felt as if I were an annoying burden, or a fly who wouldn't go away.

Sometimes when I handed my mother my report card, she'd quickly glance at it, hand it back to me, and say nothing. On more than one occasion, I did extremely well in my English classes but not so well in math and science. She never complimented me on my good grades but would instead focus on, and overblow, my poor grades. This behavior reminded me of my great-grandmother Ethel's attitude toward my grandmother.

Grandma wrote the following passage in her journal after coming home from school with a letter from the headmaster, who had requested a meeting with her mother:

I ran home as fast as I could and handed the note to my mother. On the following day, I accompanied my mother to school for the meeting, and hid behind the classroom door while the two of them spoke.

I expected to hear harsh words, because that's all I usually heard my mother use when she spoke about me. I thought the teacher would do the same, but what I heard made me cry with joy. The young teacher repeated over and over again, "She is a good child, she is a good child."

As it turned out, that teacher was the best addition to my young life. She stood by me during the entire war. She told me that, even though I was the smallest girl in the class, I was the smartest and best behaved. Summer vacation rolled around, and once again I became tortured by being around my mother all day long and being exposed to her belittling comments. I could never do right by her. I couldn't wait to go back to school. All summer long I lay on my checkered blanket writing unsent letters to my favorite teacher and prayed that I would have her for the next grade after summer vacation.

Reading this section of my grandmother's journal was heartbreaking. And, unfortunately, it resonated deep in my bones because of my own similar experiences. On one occasion—I'm unsure what grade I was in, but I'd already learned cursive writing, so I think it might have been the fourth—Mother was called to school for the quarterly parent-teacher night. Although I wasn't asked to join her, when she arrived home she shared the details of her private conference with my teacher.

I already knew I wasn't an "A" student. Like most creative children, I spent a great deal of time daydreaming and staring out the classroom window at the lush school-yard. Nature has always captivated me. Sometimes I'd look up at the sky and wonder what it would be like to be a bird or a cloud. I'd look at trees and wonder about all that they'd witnessed in their lifetime. I'd stare at flowers and imagine bees making honey from their nectar. The natural world is good for our well-being and, for me, it fosters the imagination and offers a path to freedom as well. Without naming them, and even before it was in vogue to do so, I looked to nature's spirits to provide answers to life's most challenging questions: Why am I here? What is my purpose? How can I find peace?

So, I had difficulty focusing in the classroom. I wasn't interested in what the teachers said and thought. They were simply boring. Instead of inspiring us to think, they taught us to memorize our lessons. When it came to exams, I did poorly because I continued to daydream rather than memorize.

"Diana, the teachers aren't happy with your work. You did poorly on your aptitude test," my mother said after arriving home from the school meeting. "Your teacher is concerned. She suggested you stay after school to do some remedial work."

"I hate tests, Mom. You know I never do well on them."

"Well, that's no excuse. You'll be getting tested for the rest of your life. You need to take tests seriously. You spend too much time journaling. You need to study more. Until you bring home a better report card, you're not going to be getting your weekly allowance."

My mother was rarely tactful and often confusing. Sometimes she didn't care about things, and other times she overreacted. She loved it when I felt weak or sad, and so watching me march to my bedroom crying made her feel she'd accomplished what she wanted. The new plan was that after walking home from school and having a small snack that I had prepared myself, I was to go back to school for tutoring.

After that school meeting, Mother treated me like a "bad" kid. She also didn't encourage me to ask questions; thus, in a sense, she crushed my curiosity. As my father once said, "She always looks at the glass half empty rather than half full." Her shaming me shattered my self-esteem. Thank goodness my grandmother and father built it up and made me feel good about myself. When Grandma was alive, I could do no wrong.

A few months after I graduated from nursing school, my father visited Simon and me when we were living in Montreal, which was where our kids would eventually be born. I'd been working as a registered nurse caring for those who had undergone open-heart surgery. I wanted more out of the nursing profession, but I wasn't sure what it was. On the second morning of my father's visit, he and I were skimming the classified section of the local newspaper. In those days before the Internet, that was the only way to find out about job opportunities. An ad caught my eye: "Wanted: Director of Nursing for a small, chronic care hospital. Immediate availability." Something about it appealed to me. It sounded like a dream job. I loved the elderly, and I loved being in charge, but I thought there would be no way they'd hire a new graduate.

"Dad, this job sounds amazing," I said before reading it to him.

"Well, why don't you apply?" he asked, sipping his morning coffee as we sat at our glass kitchen table.

"There's no way in the world I'd get this job. I just graduated nursing school. I hardly have any experience."

"Deedle, just try. You never know."

First thing the next morning, I called the phone number in the ad. That afternoon, they called me in for an interview. The medical director took an immediate liking to me and hired me on the spot. I thanked him and went out to the car where my father waited.

"Dad, I got the job!"

"I told you! The sky's the limit. You can do anything you set your mind to."

I worked at that job for six months before getting pregnant and learning I had to go on bed rest. The good news is that I accomplished a lot during a short period of time. The former nursing director was older and had never implemented in-service education, which was a passion of mine. I had always loved teaching. They were sad to see me go and asked if I'd return after my baby was born, but I never did. I ended up staying home to raise my eldest daughter and her two subsequent siblings while being a freelance writer.

Getting hired for that position right out of nursing school gave me a huge boost of self-esteem, but my mother declined to praise me. It was hard to know what to do that would bring a smile to her face. Sometimes I felt as if I were responsible for her depression. I wonder if my grandmother felt the same about her mother's depression. In his book, *The Body Keeps the Score* (2015), Bessel van der Kolk writes about how we feel when abandoned, and so much of what he said resonated with me. For example, at school, my mind often went blank, and I stared out the window in a trancelike state, sometimes ignoring or oblivious to what was going on around me. Sometimes I couldn't feel anything in my body. Throughout my life, I've had intermittent feelings of abandonment sprinkled with feelings of fear. I wish I still had my old journals so that I could know what was going through my mind back then. Thankfully, things changed as I became older. I became a super-aware individual.

Like Grandma, I had parents who frequently fought. She wrote this in her journal about her parents' behavior:

By the time I turned nine, I wondered if one of the reasons for my mother being nervous and short-tempered was because of my parents' faltering marriage. I was just not sure why my parents constantly bickered. Each evening after dinner, as they cleared the dishes, they found something to get angry and yell about. It was usually because of a silly and insignificant issue, such as why my father did not put the garbage out on time. The bickering would sometimes continue into the night and behind their bedroom door. These arguments left Beronia [Regina's younger sister] and me with a sense of uneasiness, but finally we realized that there was little we could do to change things.

If the arguments happened during the day, my mother would sometimes retreat for quiet time to the outside porch. From her rocking chair she would stare blankly out at the main street of Kalush. Sometimes she distracted herself by mending our family's socks.

This entry in my grandmother's journal made me aware of the emotional distance among her family members and of how bad relationships can get passed down from one generation to the next. After being married for more than forty-five years now, I believe I've learned from my ancestors and have broken the chain of unhappy and dysfunctional relationships.

As a young woman, my grandmother pondered what she wanted to do when she grew up. She shared an unforgettable story about her mother's perspective on this question. In Grandma's childhood home there was a wooden front porch with two green rocking chairs. She'd often find her parents there early in the morning or before dinner.

When Grandma was eleven, a few days before her mother died from cholera, she called her four children, one by one, to meet her on the porch. I wonder if she had a premonition of her impending death because she was already feeling ill. Grandma was scared because the last time she had been called to the porch her mother had scolded her about something she'd done wrong.

First, her mother called her oldest brother, Willy, who was nineteen. He walked out with his arms crossed across his chest, expecting the worst. He stood about four feet from his mother.

"Willy," she said, "I've been thinking about what you kids should be when you grow up. You, my son, shall be a clerk. You're very good with handling money and finances. I think this type of work will bring you much happiness in your life. Now, carry on and get your little sister and brother. I also have some news for them."

Willy walked back inside the house, not sure what to make of the news and why she had chosen this moment to share her thoughts.

The next to be called was Herman, who was seventeen. He stepped onto the porch and walked with trepidation toward his mother. He also stood about four feet away from her.

"Herman, you, my son, shall become some sort of merchant. You have a way with people, and you're a good salesman. When you were a little boy and we had a small store, you always asked to stand behind the counter to help—the customers all wanted to buy from you. You have that kind of personality. You make people laugh with your jokes. Yes, a merchant. That's what I see for you," she said.

Next came Regina's younger and only sister, Beronia, who was seven.

"I think the best thing for you, my daughter, is to be a housewife. You're so helpful in the kitchen and in tidying up the house. You'll make someone a good wife one day and will surely be a good mother. You have so much patience with those little dolls we bought you last year for your birthday." Beronia slowly walked back into the house, minding each footstep.

Next, my grandmother was called. She wondered if she was going to hear once again how her mother never wanted her and how useless she was. She believed she was her mother's least favorite child, so she suspected she'd have the worst career suggestion for her. She walked gingerly to join her mother on the porch.

"And you, Regina. What can I say about a girl who's so clumsy in the house, always breaking things?"

My grandmother stood paralyzed, waiting to hear her mother's next words.

"It perhaps shall be a surprise to hear me say that you have the potential to go the furthest of your brothers and sister. You're such a clever child. You're always reading and studying, and you always have a book in your hand. The kitchen, my dear, is not for you. You're very good with people; I've noticed that people tend to like you. You surely need to get out into the world and do some good. For you, I think you should become a doctor. Just think how many people you could help."

In her journal, my grandmother said she was completely shocked to hear her mother's words. At first, she was unsure what to do, but, as she had many times before, she defaulted to her instincts and ran to her mother to give her a hug of gratitude. She wrote that her mother held her for a brief moment and then pushed her away, looking Regina in the eyes and saying, "This doesn't excuse you from your given household responsibilities. You need to know that, Regina, so run along. The table must be set for dinner, and the clothes need to be taken down from the clothesline and folded, and that's still your job."

"Yes, Mama." Regina walked away smiling but was careful not to show her delight.

Hearing what my great-grandmother Ethel had said left me feeling happy for Grandma, especially since those were her mother's last words—words that lived in her for the rest of her life. It felt as if Ethel was finally able to admit something good about my grandmother. That her last words were positive ones was a blessing.

I would have loved to have known what my grandmother was thinking in that moment as she left the porch. I never got a chance to ask her because I learned about this scenario only from her journal after she had died. Her mother's words surely left an indelible mark given that, about a decade after arriving in the United States, Regina applied to the New York University School of Medicine. She was accepted but couldn't attend because she didn't have the tuition funds. In the 1960s, women weren't often welcomed into medical schools, and scholarships were rarely, if at all, available to them. It could be said that she was simply born a few years too early.

The power of poignant words spoken by someone who is important to us cannot be overemphasized. My encouraging father had told me that the sky was the limit in terms of what I could accomplish, and the words of my sixth-grade English teacher had subconsciously inspired me even before I knew that writing would be my lifelong passion.

In English class one day, we were all working on an essay. The teacher was a fortyish blond surfer who gingerly calypso danced on his desk the last day of school. A few days before the end of the school year, while walking around the class as we were writing, he stopped, stood behind me, and glanced over my shoulder to read my essay.

I felt his presence for a few moments but was in the flow of my writing.

Finally, he tapped me on the shoulder and whispered, "Diana, you have a special command of the English language. My sense is that you're going to be a writer one day."

While it felt like a passing comment at the time, now, more than five decades later, his words still echo in my ears. So many comments and actions from our childhood stay with us and affect us for the rest of our lives. I wonder if, subconsciously, this was one of the reasons I had the confidence to pursue a writing career. It also reminds me of the importance of role models and teachers in the lives of children.

Reflections / Writing Prompts

1. Think about a teacher or adult who strongly influenced your future career choice. Describe your connection.

2. Discuss what kind of student you were and how that influenced who you are today.

3. Muse about what subjects were your favorite in school and whether your interests are still the same.

4. Reflect on your grades as a student and on your parents' reaction to good or bad grades.

5. Reflect on how your upbringing has affected the kind of parent or aunt or uncle you've become.

12 Dealing with a Long-Term Illness

It is in moments of illness that we are compelled to recognize that we live not alone but chained to a creature of a different kingdom, whole worlds apart, who has no knowledge of us and by whom it is impossible to make ourselves understood: our body.

~ Marcel Proust

In my article, "How Illness Can be Lonely and What to Do about it" (2020), I share my perspective about how isolating illness can be. The fact is that when we're dealing with short- or long-term illnesses, we are most connected to our bodies. When we feel lonely, we feel empty and drained, and we're deeply in touch with the fragility of life. During the coronavirus pandemic, many people felt lonely, and social media became a large part of their lives; but for me it fed into an already deep sense of loneliness. The only way to cope with loneliness is to force oneself to connect with others. Even when doing so, I'm unfortunately prone to loneliness, especially when I ponder being an only child and dealing with two different types of cancer.

I often think of the time I was alerted to my diagnosis of multiple myeloma, the second cancer diagnosis in five years. It was in 2006 when I went for my five-year checkup after breast cancer, and my blood work showed an abnormality.

"Your blood-protein levels are abnormally elevated, and I'd like you to return for a repeat test," my oncologist told me on the phone the week after I had had lab work done.

"What can that mean?"

"It's too early to discuss. Don't worry."

Easy for him to say.

When I hung up, I refrained from researching on the Internet because I really didn't have enough information to go on, and I didn't want to overreact unnecessarily. I prayed for a lab error. Yet, I knew Simon, the scientist, did his own quiet research and, the following morning, I could see worry on his face.

I returned for the second blood test, and the results still showed an elevated protein called immunoglobulin-A (IgA).

"I'm not sure what's going on," my oncologist told me—not a very reassuring comment to an anxious patient who was hoping to celebrate the anniversary of her five-year survival after a breast-cancer diagnosis. "We have to do further testing."

"Like what?"

"We need to do a bone-marrow biopsy to rule out multiple myeloma."

"What's that?"

After a pregnant pause—I could almost feel him cringe as he started to speak—he replied, "It's a cancer in the bone marrow of the plasma cells that are responsible for producing antibodies to help fight infection. Myeloma happens when healthy cells change and grow out of control. This suppresses the immune response."

I felt my eyes fill with tears as my mind pedaled back to five years earlier. *How could this be happening?*

"Listen, Diana, please don't worry. Let's wait and see," he added.

Still seated at the desk in my home office, I hung up the phone and stared at the Edward Hopper painting, *Compartment C Car*, on the wall in front of me. Paintings, music, and art have magical healing effects. Art is healing because it forces us to forge a connection between our mind, body, and spirit. The Hopper painting is of a woman reading on a train. I wanted to escape. I wanted to hop on the train and go far away with her. I couldn't bear any more bad news.

"Bone marrow cancer," I said out loud. "You must be kidding."

People say that there's a reason for everything, but I could not imagine a reason for this. I remember that, when I was diagnosed with breast cancer, my middle daughter was only eighteen. After putting her arm around my shoulder, she looked into my eyes and wisely said, "Mom, I see a book in this." It makes me tear up in remembering those words of a daughter who really knows and understands her mother.

In slow motion, I transported myself to my reading chair and ruminated about how something could possibly be wrong with me again. I wondered about the idea that my body remembered some of my childhood trauma, not only of losing my grandmother but also of the verbal abuse I encountered with my mother. I suddenly became disappointed in my body. I'd survived breast cancer and was glad to be alive, but, in many ways, because I'd lost a breast, I didn't feel whole. Each day when I got dressed, I was reminded of my scarred landscape—three Caesareans and a mastectomy and reconstruction.

I played gentle, spiritual music in the background, something I've often done to raise my vibration and bring me in tune with myself and my spirit. I was sitting at my desk, and a ladybug landed on my right hand. She flew in through my open office door. It was a magical moment. I didn't know what the message was, but something inside me knew that everything was going to be okay and that I was to set out on an unknown journey.

Much to my dismay, and as I have recounted earlier, the biopsy revealed smoldering myeloma, an early precursor of the disease that—lacking physical symptoms—didn't yet necessitate treatment. This cancer has treatments but no cure. I'd have to live with it for the rest of my life. Unlike a malignant tumor in the breast, it couldn't be excised.

At the time, none of my children were married, nor did they have permanent partners. However, they were all living on their own. I expressed my concern to my husband about never being able to meet my grandchildren. This possibility deeply saddened me, particularly since I'd had such a great relationship with my own grandmother, which I wanted to emulate.

I mused about my father-in-law's comment after my first cancer diagnosis: "Have no fear, Diana, have no fear." Like my father, he was a Holocaust survivor who'd lost his parents and siblings and lived through a difficult immigrant experience. He knew how important it was to have no fear.

My first course of action was to connect with a Los Angeles integrative internist to formulate a plan to increase my immunity with supplements and vitamins. He'd recently had a myeloma patient who was being treated by Dr. Kevin (not his actual name), who, at the time, practiced at the Mayo Clinic. The internist suggested I make an appointment. Dr. Kevin was a brilliant myeloma researcher and saw only a select number of patients. I was a fascinating case because it was rare for a woman in her early fifties to have myeloma—a disease common in older men, particularly those who worked in the coal industry.

From our first meeting in 2007, Dr. Kevin and I have had a great connection. He's smart and intuitive, and I trust him. On a few occasions, he gave medical talks in our community, and my husband and I had him over for dinner.

For fourteen years, we made biannual trips to The Mayo Clinic. Because it is a research facility, they took many vials of blood for research. It was important for me to become well hydrated the day before so that my veins wouldn't collapse.

Dr. Kevin had a conservative, "watch and see" approach. "No point treating unnecessarily," he told me.

I also learned that there's no textbook treatment for this type of cancer. Each situation is different. I was confident in my multiple-myeloma team. I believed we could keep my myeloma smoldering unless my body had another plan, which I wouldn't know for many years to come.

~ ~ ~

It's fascinating that my diagnosis of ductal carcinoma was an early precursor of full-blown breast cancer, just as my smoldering myeloma was a precursor of myeloma itself. Was my body giving me messages by subjecting me to these two precursor forms of cancer? Were they warning signs telling me to take better care of myself? It was hard *not* to read into these messages. Years later, my naturopath said, "It's quite amazing that you've had two 'almost' cancers." That certainly inspired me to stop and think about his words.

Studies have shown that half of those with smoldering myeloma develop myeloma within five years. Thankfully, I wasn't in that group. Some patients live for many years without requiring myeloma treatment. When I was diagnosed, the recommended treatments had multiple side effects, but new treatments are emerging with less serious ones. Dr. Kevin said that if I waited long enough, new, more targeted and refined treatments would become available. Since I had no physical symptoms such as anemia, broken bones, or kidney disease, his plan made sense to me. Isn't it true that we stick with the physicians whose philosophies align with our own?

I'm also a believer that, while medicine is a science, diagnosis and treatment are more of an art. I learned this from my mother, who worked for years as a medical assistant, and from my own short career as a registered nurse.

In 2012, six years after my diagnosis, I decided to connect with a local oncologist, just in case I would need treatment in the future. I went in for annual follow-up appointments. On my visit early in the pandemic, she suggested that I begin monthly intravenous immunotherapy to increase my immunity as a precaution against the coronavirus. This suggestion resonated with me, knowing that I had a reduced number of efficient antibodies that could attack the potentially deadly virus.

Some specialists don't believe immunotherapy affects myeloma-marker numbers, while others think it does. It's always challenging for the patient when there are differing opinions. That's when I revert to Grandma's teachings about following my intuition.

After checking with Dr. Kevin in early 2020 I decided to begin immunotherapy. Once a month for six months, I masked, went to the local clinic, and sat in a reclining chair for five hours in the cancer unit to receive immunoglobulin infusions from an unknown person. Although I was assured of its safety and that the immunoglobulin was screened, I still questioned the long-term effects.

In May 2020, Dr. Kevin wrote me an email saying he was leaving the Mayo Clinic and returning to Canada, to be the medical director of a prominent cancer center. I was happy for him but devastated for myself. Who would care for me in the same way for the duration of my disease? How could I find someone else who aligned with my philosophy?

"Can you recommend a hematologist/oncologist in Los Angeles?" I asked.

"Well, there are a couple. Remember, everyone has different ideas about treating this disease. There's someone at Cedars-Sinai and at the City of Hope."

"Since Cedars-Sinai Hospital is closer to me, I'll go with that one. Would you be able to speak with him and give a personal referral? I feel like a lost puppy."

"No problem. We've done some research together. We're familiar."

I said goodbye to Dr. Kevin and wished him well. He told me to keep in touch and to call if I ever needed him.

The thought of getting to know a new physician was daunting and scary. While waiting for my first appointment with my new oncologist, I pondered what his treatment plan would be.

Prior to our call, his office sent a blood-draw requisition. I found a nurse who did home visits and drew blood. I'd already received four months of immunotherapy. Unlike the Mayo Clinic, which immediately posted blood test results online, Cedars-Sinai only allowed me to see the results after the physician had reviewed them. Soaked in anxiety, I waited two long weeks for my new oncologist to share my results.

In June 2020 we had our first telemedicine call. We did the usual introductions, and I told him that Simon was listening on speaker phone.

"I have all your records, and I've spoken to your previous oncologist about you. I have a good sense of where you're at. I did notice that your numbers have been climbing. Perhaps you're gearing up for treatment," the new oncologist said in a cavalier tone.

I couldn't believe the timing. I froze, not knowing what to say. I had been in remission for fourteen years, and now, just after my old oncologist had left for Canada, I suddenly needed treatment? I felt jinxed by Dr. Kevin's departure. Something didn't make sense. How could this be happening?

"Interesting," I said. "I wonder why the sudden shift?"

"Myeloma is just like that. It can shift to the point where you need treatment. Anyway, I like staying ahead of the curve," the doctor added.

I remember hearing that this new oncologist was a little more proactive regarding treatment. It seemed he wasn't even curious about investigating possible reasons for the sudden elevation in the myeloma-marker numbers.

"Do you know I began monthly immunotherapy a few months ago? Could that possibly be a contributing factor? What about all the wine I've been drinking during quarantine? What about my new collagen supplements? Could any of those be contributing?" I was desperate to find a reason for why the marker numbers were elevated. I did not want to believe that my myeloma was becoming full blown.

I sat on the sofa with the speaker phone nearby, impatient for him to say "yes."

"I don't believe there's a correlation with any of these things. Many of my patients are on immunotherapy, and I've not seen any change in their blood work," he said.

In fear and wonder, my husband and I looked at one another. How could this be so sudden? We had not even *met* this oncologist, so we hadn't had time to build trust in him. He was the chairman of the myeloma department at a large urban hospital—but still. I felt like I'd lost my closest ally in Dr. Kevin but recalled him telling me to keep in touch. I wanted to bombard him with questions, but how much would be too much?

My instincts told me it wasn't time to begin treatment. The next day, outside my writing studio, a hummingbird came to my feeder filled with red-colored water. She hovered for only a few moments but longer than usual. She must have known I needed her. I glanced at the photo of my grandmother on my desk and thanked her for the visitation. I asked her again what she thought.

"Follow your instincts. You have good ones," she reminded me.

To confirm my feelings, I sent a short email to Dr. Kevin, and he concurred. He also suggested stopping immunotherapy.

"Beginning immunotherapy is the only thing that changed since your last blood test. Let's see if it didn't throw things off. Yes, your light chains [one of the myeloma markers] have increased. Why don't you stop immunotherapy for at least six months and let's see what happens?" he wrote.

I was in a quandary, unsure what to tell my new oncologist. I didn't know how he'd react if he knew I was consulting with my old oncologist, although I think he already knew I was.

"I've decided to stop immunotherapy and will do all I can *not* to expose myself to COVID-19," I said two months later during our next telemedicine call.

"That's fine. As I said before, I just want to stay ahead of the curve, which is why I'm suggesting treatment. But if you're not ready, that's okay. Treatment works better if the patient believes in it."

I thought that was an interesting comment, and I liked that he thought so, because even if I began chemotherapy, there was a chance it wouldn't work. So why start now?

"If you want to wait on chemotherapy, why don't we do some blood work every two months instead of every six? I don't want to miss anything."

"Sounds like a plan," I said and thanked him for his time.

Lo and behold, my blood tests two months later revealed that my myeloma-marker numbers had dropped slightly! I couldn't help but think that wasn't a coincidence. Sometimes, we must be our own best doctor. I remain optimistic. Because myeloma is incurable, if I ever begin treatment, chances are I'll have to continue with various drug cocktails and other therapy modalities for the rest of my life. I also remember hearing years ago, "If you begin treatment too early, there's a chance you'll get rid of all the cancer cells, but the good cells might get upset and start to act up." This made sense to me. At the time I was a young, sixty-eight-year-old woman. I felt good and wasn't ready to give up. And though it might not be wholly fair to say so, that's what entering treatment felt like to me.

A month later, when I saw my gynecologist for my annual exam, I told her about not wanting to begin treatment. As an empath, she stopped for a moment before responding. She and my internist had been colleagues, so she knew I preferred the integrative approach to medicine. She'd followed me for years and was someone whom I deeply admired. Plus, she had good instincts.

"I don't know much about myeloma, but I do know your bone density has dipped; you have what we call osteopenia," she said after seeing the results of my biannual DEXA scan. "This isn't uncommon for a woman your age, but please ask your oncologist in case it has something to do with the myeloma. In the meantime, I'd like you to read *How Not to Die* by Dr. Michael Greger (2015). He's brilliant and speaks about every health ailment and the importance of a vegan diet. As I told you a long time ago, stay away from cheeses and chicken—but he has even more to offer in his book."

"Thank you," I said, changing back into my clothes.

While standing at the counter waiting to check out, I ordered the book on Amazon for next-day delivery.

When it arrived, I began reading and couldn't put it down. I was hooked on the first page. "It all started with my grandmother," Greger wrote on the first page of the book's preface.

I kept reading about how he, like me, had been influenced by his grandmother. As it turned out, he was inspired to become a physician because his grandmother, at the age of sixty-five, had developed end-stage heart disease and was given a death sentence until she stumbled upon dietary and lifestyle changes, which had added another thirty-one years to her life.

In addition to the chapter on heart disease, Greger devotes one chapter each to several ailments and recommends the best diet and lifestyle changes for each disease. This was the first trade book I'd seen that had an entire chapter devoted to blood cancers—and a section on multiple myeloma! "Multiple myeloma is one of the most dreaded cancers," he wrote (p. 159).

In addition to being a huge advocate of a vegan diet, he suggests regular doses of curcumin, which can stop the growth of myeloma cells. Of course, many of the studies on this plant-based supplement are short term, and only time will reveal its efficacy. I was already on this supplement, so felt as if I were on the right track.

After one month on a vegan diet, I was due for my next blood work. The anxiety over these tests is overwhelming for both my husband and me. Thankfully, my numbers remained the same. While I would have loved to see them drop, I'm glad they didn't increase. I don't want to jinx the situation, but I'm continuing this course. If a diet shift was good enough for Greger's grandmother, why wouldn't it be good enough for me?

After reading Greger's book and buying the accompanying cookbook, I continue to get creative with the vegan diet. I've had fewer food cravings and achieved some desired weight loss. My body feels healthier and stronger, and I live in hope that my next results show improved numbers. I'm determined to keep my myeloma smoldering.

After nearly a year in quarantine, I was anxious to get my vaccine. By the end of 2022, over one million Americans had died from COVID-19, and the transmission news was terrifying. There had been contradictory reports, much misinformation, and many unknowns about the evolution of this virus and its variants. I felt called to volunteer in some medical capacity. I inquired about how to get relicensed and assist in the vaccination programs, but it would have been an arduous process. Instead, I signed up with the Medical Reserve Corps to volunteer at the vaccination clinics managed by the local public-health department.

After working two shifts, I was entitled to get my vaccine. By mid-February 2021, and within six weeks of working, I'd already had both doses of the Moderna vaccine. Initially, I was set on getting the Pfizer vaccine because the company was established and had more patents than Moderna, which, until the pandemic, had never received an FDA-approved patent. However, my oncologist said I should try to get any vaccine I could because I needed protection as soon as possible.

Being on a vegan diet and getting the vaccine has been empowering, providing me with some control over my health and well-being. What's been equally important is listening to Grandma's messages about the importance of being conscious and following my instincts. I'm so grateful for her wise-woman teachings. I'm also thankful for other offerings from the pandemic, which taught me lessons that made her teachings even more relevant.

I should add that, at the time of this writing, now some months later, after speaking with my naturopath it was decided that I needed more protein in my diet. We lose muscle mass as we age, and only exercise and protein can bring it back. Thus, I am a pescatarian with one exception. The acupuncturist whom I see on a biweekly basis is a big advocate of bone broth for multiple myeloma. He suggests one cup a day. I go to the butcher to get fresh bones and fill my freezer up with jars of bone broth that—in addition to the bones—has been made from an array of vegetables that are strained out after two hours of cooking.

Reflections / Writing Prompts

1. Are you or anyone you know dealing with a long-term or chronic illness? If yes, share your story.

2. How have you dealt with illness or disease during different life stages?

3. Have you ever had an experience in which your medical opinion differed from those of your health-care provider? If yes, how did you deal with it?

4. Have you ever had some unexpected sightings of animals or birds during difficult times?

5. Have you read a medical or health book that inspires you and that provides advice you follow?

13 How Life Gives Us Perspective

There are always flowers for those who want to see them.
~ Henri Matisse

Many of my blogs and articles make some reference to the importance of perspective. As young children, we have little perspective because we've lived only a short while. I tell my students that writing a memoir during one's adolescence or twenties is a tough challenge because one of the most compelling aspects of writing a memoir is the ability to look back on our lives and reflect about our lived experiences. While writing about those experiences is important, what's most important is writing about how we reacted to them and how they affected the person we've become.

We're all transformed by our experiences, but traumatic experiences bring even more dramatic transformation. I'll be forever changed by living through a pandemic. My grandmother was forever changed by living through the cholera pandemic and being orphaned at the age of eleven. In addition, my father's life was forever changed by being a Holocaust survivor, and my life was forever changed by knowing their stories and by my own experiences, including raising a family and my cancer journeys.

Mental-health challenges are universal, and we all cope differently. Some people are more resilient than others. However, when I reflect on my father's experience of the

Holocaust, I wonder how he survived. His saving grace was his positive attitude and the gratitude he felt to be alive. He was deeply thankful that he was able to emigrate to the United States. His way of being taught me many things.

For five of my father's most formative years—from ages fifteen to twenty—he was a prisoner at Nazi Germany's Dachau concentration camp. He ate scraps of left-behind food and, at night, slept on a wooden pallet with hundreds of others, shivering under thin blankets. But no matter what horrible things he witnessed and endured, he never lost hope. He taught me the power of hope and how we can help one another obtain it.

A few years before my father died at the age of seventy-one from congestive heart failure (after coughing up blood from three decades of cigarette smoking), my husband asked him about the scar on his forehead.

"That scar was from 'the camp.' You know, I worked in the kitchen peeling potatoes. I was one of the lucky ones. I got a kitchen job because the Nazi who ran it knew my father owned a well-respected lumberyard. One day, when I was peeling a potato, I left a little more of the potato on the peel than I was supposed to, and I tossed it to the prisoners behind me in the barracks. When a Nazi soldier saw me do this, he hit my forehead with the butt of his rifle."

"No good deed goes unpunished," my father later told me. He said his actions were worth the scar. He was the type of person who walked the streets of New York City tossing coins from his pocket to the homeless.

He used to ask his miserly brother, Bob, "Why are you so stingy? Will they sew your money into your shroud?"

Still, the war left my father with lifelong physical and psychological scars. For example, he couldn't tolerate the sight of red meat because, during the war, he saw too many dead bodies. "The sight of blood just turns my stomach," he used to tell me.

My father shared how he witnessed his oldest brother, Joshua, and his mother being taken from their ghetto apartment in Koenigsberg by the Nazis. They were herded onto a train and transported to the gas chambers to their untimely deaths. He and Bob were the only survivors in their family.

After the Holocaust, most Jews turned either toward or against religion. Bob turned to religion, but my father turned against it. He believed that religion divides people instead of uniting them. However, he wanted to honor the religion of his ancestors, so he graciously joined his brother on holy Jewish holidays. He wasn't a practicing Jew, nor was my mother.

Six million Jews perished in the Holocaust. My father said if there were a God, he or she wouldn't have allowed the killing of so many people. Long before *compassion* was even a buzzword, he lived a life of compassion and loving kindness, and that became his religion. He taught me how to walk the high road. When people were mean or unkind, he taught me how important it was to respond to them with love. He was grateful for his freedom and hopeful for humanity. This attitude has served me well, especially during this pandemic.

~ ~ ~

Living through the COVID-19 pandemic has given me a new perspective. I have realized the fragility of life and the importance of interconnectedness. Like many others, I've reorganized my priorities. So far, we've lost more Americans to the coronavirus than in any conflict since the Civil War. In the early months of the pandemic, we heard talk about how it would be the great equalizer. It would take down and humble all manner of people. That's not a nice thought. We weren't prepared for this. Now, people are still dying. People are still mourning. People are still dealing with physical, financial, and mental-health challenges leading in extreme cases to trauma and even suicide. Much of our collective sense of well-being has been sacrificed. Studies have shown that even those who recover after the pandemic may be at increased risk for a depressive episode in their future.

The quarantine, which lasted over a year, has taken a psychological toll on many people. Humans are, by nature, social creatures. Losing our connection with others adds to our suffering. I wouldn't be surprised if the next pandemic is one of mental health, and I wonder if we're prepared.

Loneliness, anxiety, stress, and depression are feelings commonly shared both by those who fear getting COVID-19 as well as by those who have ended up getting the virus—with all the physical challenges that entails. Those who've lost loved ones have also suffered immense mental-health challenges, especially if they were unable to be with their loved ones as they passed or have the usual funeral ceremony to honor them.

The unemployment rates have been unprecedented, unseen even in the Great Depression of my grandmother's time. We don't yet know how the pandemic has permanently affected our brains, our society, and our ways of being.

While most of us have accepted this new reality and realize that the virus will be around for a long time, nearly all of us have had to make various shifts in our lives. Those who have been most challenged by the pandemic typically don't adapt well to change and tend to crave social connections. As a writer who spends a lot of time alone, I have simply been offered more of the same kind of isolation. But writers can't write in a vacuum; we need experiences and human companionship for inspiration and support. We need to people watch and connect with friends and colleagues to nurture our creativity.

I spent most of my pandemic time living in the moment, accepting the situation, watching everything unfold. I knew that panicking wouldn't help the pandemic end more quickly. In the early months, it was nice to be part of a simpler lifestyle. The restaurants were closed, so Simon and I became masterful cooks. I bought a few cookbooks, and we learned new recipes. My middle daughter and her family moved in with us for four months, and my son and his soon-to-be wife also moved in. Being with children was a constant reminder of how to live in the moment.

For some people, the not-knowing aspect of the pandemic—when it will end and how life will be when it does—resulted in waves of anxiety. This wasn't the case for me. Having two of my children and their loved ones move in with us was a cause for celebration. We had the opportunity to get to know one another all over again. We hadn't lived together for at least a decade. It took some getting used to, but we decided to make it fun and call it our little Commune Raab. Everybody helped.

The time together also provided an opportunity for reflection and contemplation. It was a time for deep thought about what was important to us, and it also reminded us of our mortality. It was a time to think about beginnings and endings. I thought about how many loved ones I'd lost over the past six decades, beginning with my beloved grandmother and then my best friend, Nancy, who—when I was twelve—got hit by a car when we went to the movies one night. Next to pass was my grandfather and then my nursing mentor and friend, Lynda, who jumped off a thirteen-story building. After that, my father; my friend, Thom Steinbeck; and then my writing mentor and colleague, Phil, all died—and, during the pandemic, my teenage boyfriend, Philip. Through social media, I learned that a few other childhood friends had also passed away.

I wrote about and honored each of them—who they were and what I'd learned from them. The constant thread in my life has always been love. I've always been able to surround myself with those who loved and appreciated me.

I thought about how sometimes people leave us suddenly, without warning, and how difficult it is not to have a sense of closure. I'd been fortunate; I was able to say goodbye to almost all those I've lost except for my maternal and paternal grandparents. My father's parents died in the Holocaust, so unfortunately I never had a chance to meet them. I mused about how my grandmother, Regina, never had an opportunity to say goodbye to her mother, Ethel, before Ethel was taken away to the infirmary to die. I can't imagine how Regina felt.

Just as I didn't begin missing my grandmother until I was in my forties, I wonder if she only began missing her mother at the same age. Maybe that's one of the reasons Grandma took her own life.

~ ~ ~

About six months into the coronavirus pandemic, I received a call from the night nurse at my mother's assisted-living facility. Whenever the facility's name comes up on my iPhone screen, I freeze, fearing my mother has died. I wasn't expecting what I heard.

"Hi, Diana, this is Stephanie, your mother's nurse. I had to call to tell you that your mother tested positive for COVID, and we need to put her in isolation."

"Oh, no!" I responded, knowing Mother must have acquired it from the staff because she had no visitors. I was disappointed that they weren't more careful.

"That's awful. Does she have any symptoms?" I asked.

"She's just very tired and weak, but we're keeping an eye on her. We'll let you know if anything changes."

"Is it possible to FaceTime with her or speak with her?" I asked, fearing I might not hear her voice again. It had already been eighteen months since I'd visited.

"She's sleeping now and quite weak, but I'll tell her that we spoke," Stephanie said.

"Does she have a fever?"

"No, but as you know, seniors don't always get fevers because their bodies don't fight the virus in the same way."

"Okay. Thank you for calling, Stephanie. Please keep in touch. It's so frustrating that I can't visit her."

"I understand. Please call any time."

My mother had been living in the facility for about three years. We received monthly newsletters from the administration with community updates. They began COVID-19 quarantine in mid-March 2020 and maintained a strict protocol for staff and residents. Visitors were no longer allowed into the building. They diligently kept everybody safe, but, unfortunately, the week before all the residents were to receive the vaccine, my mother and fifteen other residents tested positive. The timing couldn't have been worse. For the first eight months of quarantine, there were no reports of any residents having COVID-19, but, in the latest newsletter, I noticed there were at least a dozen cases.

The next day, Stephanie phoned back.

"Diana, it's Stephanie again. Unfortunately, your mother took a turn for the worse. She started coughing quite hard during the night. We have to call an ambulance and get her to the hospital. I think she needs oxygen, and we can't look after her here."

I felt as if my heart skipped a beat. It seemed likely that I had seen my mother for the last time. How could an elderly, overweight woman survive this virus? I felt a desperate need to hear her voice and see her face. I became frightened. There were so many things I wanted to tell my mother before she moved on. I knew there was no way to see her or speak to her. My frustration became elevated, even though I was able to remain calm on the phone.

"I'm so sorry to hear this. Please give her my love and let her know I'm sending healing wishes."

"Will do."

I hung up and began to journal. I then went to my card drawer for a get-well card and immediately sent one to her in a priority-mail envelope, praying that she'd have a chance to read it or have somebody read it to her.

My mother has always had a resilient constitution. Over the course of her lifetime, she's fallen off her horse at least a dozen times, and she's survived concussions and multiple broken bones. She's taken antibiotics maybe three times in her entire life. She nursed her colds with sleep and drinking lots of fluids. She's had dental surgery without Novocaine, and at ninety she took only one pill for hypertension. Regardless of her strength, I was concerned about the toll this virus would take on her.

I've always managed to maintain the practice of being the best daughter. Since my father died in 1991, I've been attentive to Mother's care, sending flowers, fruit from our fruit trees, and photos of her children and grandchildren. Unfortunately, there has never been a nod of gratitude except from the staff at the facility.

A few weeks after my mother moved into the facility, the social worker, Julie, and I had a long phone chat.

I was sitting at my desk looking into my grandmother's eyes in her photograph. "Julie, I'm so frustrated. I try to do the best for my mother, but she's so ungrateful and mean to me. She told other staff members and me that she's mad at me for selling her house and putting her in a facility. She said she never wants to see me again."

"Diana, this sometimes happens, and you shouldn't worry about it. All of us here know you're a wonderful and caring daughter. She's not an easy person, and we're doing our best."

For a moment, I channeled my grandmother, and a hummingbird appeared at the feeder hanging from the tree outside my office window. It fluttered for a few moments, took some nectar, and then—I swear—looked into my eyes before it flew away. That was Grandma again, telling me to let everything go. My mother would be okay, but I still wanted to finish voicing my thoughts to Julie.

"It really bothers my husband how much she hurts me. To protect myself, he suggests I don't call her anymore. That's hard for me; I'm an only child. What's more, my three kids really don't want anything to do with her because she's also not nice to them."

"You need to take care of yourself, Diana. Leave her in our hands."

"Thanks, Julie, you're so comforting."

"Anytime, Diana."

I got up from my desk to tell my husband about the phone call, and he agreed with what Julie had said.

"I need a glass of wine," I told him.

Together we walked into the kitchen, hand in hand, and toasted my mother and the letting go of my fear.

The following morning, Julie sent this email:

I understand the dynamics and fully agree with you and your husband. I don't think you have opposing views. Maintaining the relationship with strong boundaries is the way to protect yourself. You have a deep regard for "motherhood," as defined by you, not your mother. You continue to care because of who you are. You're building and defining this attitude, giving this life sustenance on your terms.

I felt extremely grateful for being understood.

Prior to the beginning of the pandemic, I would have been petrified to hear that my mother had been taken to a hospital. And though I was deeply concerned, I maintained a calm center, trusting that the universe would take care of everything. Also, as a grandmother of five, I had little time to worry over that which I could not control.

Although I've always been a spiritual person, the pandemic inspired me to further deepen my practice. I took online courses, set daily intentions, meditated, lit candles, and regularly refreshed my altar, where I placed photos of those who needed a little extra attention from the universe, my mother included. I exited the reactive phase of my life and entered the acceptance phase. I also accepted my mother's life—an acceptance that I realized the day I called her after she returned from the hospital. I kept in mind a comment she'd made a few months earlier when my cousin had asked her if she was depressed: "I've just lived too long."

The day of the phone call, I was at my desk thumbing through stationery catalogs. I came upon some greeting cards with hummingbirds on the front. I wondered if they were a message from my grandmother and what she was trying to tell me. I glanced at her photo and got the message that I should probably call to see how my mother was feeling after returning to the facility.

"Welcome back," I said. "I bet you're happy to be recovered from the virus."

"What virus?"

"You were in the hospital with COVID-19, the virus everyone's been talking about for the past nine months."

"Really? I must have been asleep the entire time. I don't remember a thing."

"You were there for two weeks, and then they sent you to arehab facility for another three weeks."

"No kidding. That's news to me."

I sat shocked at her comment. Was it possible she didn't remember anything? Was that normal? I remembered learning in nursing school about something called hospital psychosis, and I imagined that's what my mother was suffering from. I felt bad for her but, at the same time, thought that maybe it was a blessing she had missed out on all the chaos.

"Well, anyway, have a good day, and I'll call you again soon," I said.

"Okay," she said.

When I hung up, I was struck by a sharp awareness of the passage of time. I thought of my mother—the horseback rider who used to take me to the stable and have me sit in the back seat with the manure she brought home to fertilize her garden, the woman who had ten green thumbs and gave her plants and horse more attention than she gave me—and realized it was time to let go of all that, time to come to peace with myself, time to finally gain a sense of resolve.

It took me a long time to get there, and challenges have remained. After one of my mother's antagonizing calls in which she once again told me she was angry that I'd sold her house, I phoned my spiritual counselor, Susan. She gave me powerful guidance.

I usually schedule my phone calls with Susan when I have at least two hours alone without disturbance. As a spiritual counselor, she connects with spirit to help people deal with their life challenges. Her sessions usually lasted about an hour or more. Sometimes I set up sessions in advance, but she was terrific about being available during crisis times like these. When she can, she tries to fit her clients in almost immediately.

When I got on the phone, I told her about the last call with my mother.

"Diana, you've been dealing with this for a long time. Let's think about how I can support you through it." After several moments of silent contemplation, she said, "You know, I have an idea that can help you. How would you feel about burying her spirit?"

"Burying her spirit? How would I do that? She's still alive."

"Yes, I know, but it would be a ritual."

"Honestly, I'm open to any ideas. I can't take these phone calls anymore. Of course, I don't want anything to happen to her, but I'm emotionally drained," I said, feeling tears flood my eyes as happened so often when I spoke about Mother.

"Okay, let's talk about the possibilities."

"Go ahead."

"What I want you to do is get a small box and put things inside that remind you of her. If you're up to it, write her a letter and include that also."

"Wow. Okay. Then what?"

"You live near the beach, right?"

"I do."

"I want you to take the box to the beach, bury it, and then have a short ceremony. Burying her spirit will free you from her—even though she's physically alive, her spirit will be dead."

"That seems like a hard thing to do. Could it backfire?"

"No way. I think it will serve you well."

The next day, I wrote my mother a simple, two-page letter thanking her for bringing me into this world. I thanked her for buying me my first journal and taking me to the library every week. I thanked her for arranging my trip to Canada where I met Simon, which changed my life forever. I told her I had tried to be a good daughter to no avail. I said I was sorry that she remained mad at me for putting her in an assisted-living facility. I said I knew how much she enjoyed her freedom, but she could no longer live alone, and I had had no choice but to find a safe place for her. I told her I loved her and wished her a peaceful journey.

In the box, I put the letter, a few feathers, a photo of her and her horse, and a smattering of geranium flowers, which were her favorite. I asked a dear friend, who knew my mother, if she'd join me for the beach ceremony, and she graciously agreed.

We went to the nearby beach and, halfway between the bluffs and the ocean, I dug a hole for the box with my hands. We buried it together and then found a little tree to plant beside it as a marker. I looked at the bluffs, making an effort to remember the spot in case I wanted to visit it in the future. I cried, and my friend held me close. Doing this ritual gave me relief from a long-term burden. I breathed deeply and slowly walked back to the car. My friend spent the night and, over dinner, we toasted my mother.

And now, as we enter what I hope is the pandemic's final throes, and as my mother's spirit rests in that box by the sea, I feel at peace. Like Grandma, I understand what it takes to be a warrior and to keep on giving against all odds.

Love has indeed held me together, and I shall never change.

Reflections /Writing Prompts

1. What adult experience have you had that has given you an added perspective on your life?

2. Have you had any experiences that you now consider to be very lucky?

3. Reflect on your connection to religion and spirituality.

4. Discuss what challenges the pandemic has caused for you and your loved ones.

5. What coping mechanisms or self-care methods do you turn to when under stress?

14 Conscious Living and Transcendence

As we grow in our consciousness, there will be more compassion and much more love, and then the barriers between people, between religions, between nations, will begin to fall. Yes, we have to beat down the separateness.

~ Ram Dass

The events of our childhoods have the power to shape our lives and linger for a lifetime. They can build character and be the guiding light for finding our personal path. Sometimes childhood experiences establish themes that follow us into adulthood. Perhaps one of these experiences was a joyful one, or maybe it was related to trauma or pain as a result of loss, abandonment, being orphaned, or being severely physically or emotionally hurt.

We all respond differently to challenging life experiences. Some people are blessed to be able to turn disorder into order, to make good from bad, and to draw meaning from lived experiences. The ability to do this could be viewed as grace, but, unfortunately, there are those who live with unresolved childhood wounds for the rest of their lives.

Abuse and neglect are the most common forms of wounds or adverse childhood experiences (ACEs). Emotional and physical abandonment, which is what I felt when my grandmother took her life, is also becoming more and more of a problem.

During my decades of storytelling and helping others write their memoirs, and from my work as a research psychologist, I've come to learn that those who've survived challenging or traumatic childhoods tend to be more conscious and intuitive. In fact, these characteristics have helped them survive. My grandmother, father, and I have fallen into this category. When you're exposed to someone who is highly conscious, you feel an energy jolt from them. You feel a deep connection. You might sense a field of greater awareness.

My deep sense of awareness had its roots during childhood. Being raised by two hardworking parents who did not follow any particular spiritual or religious practice left me with a lot of time by myself to wonder. Journaling became my spiritual practice, and that's where I explored life purpose and life passions. During my weekly visits to the library, I went straight to the biography section, for I thought that reading stories about real-life people would help me explore how to live and what type of person I wanted to be. We rarely had family conversations in which this type of subject was discussed. Life was either about work or play, rarely inquiry. Biographies and memoirs, in addition to poetry, continue to be my favorite genres.

As a result of my lifelong experiences, my life has also been marked by being a seeker. If you are at a crossroads, or if your life path has also been that of a seeker, chances are that you'll ask questions about your life purpose, your destiny, and how you can discover it. These are indeed sacred questions. They're awakening questions that will inspire you to look for the messages elicited by your heart, which will compel you to examine what matters most to you.

In her book *Women Rowing North*, Mary Pipher (2019) says, "At seventy, I am more content with my life as it is. Many nights I go to sleep thinking that if this were the last day on Earth for me, I would be happy with how I spent it.

If I knew I only had one week to live, I don't believe I would change much on my schedule" (p. 227). As I myself approach seventy, I feel the same sentiments. I'm proud of my accomplishments and of how I live each and every day.

Through my passion for writing, I've been able to express myself and write my personal story. I figured out how to embrace a new level of self-worth, in addition to transcending into a deeper sense of consciousness. For me, this has involved proving to myself that I was capable of certain achievements such as an advanced education. Thus, when I was forty-nine, I received my MFA and, by the time I was sixty-one—the age at which Grandma took her life— I'd received my doctorate in transpersonal psychology.

Since childhood, I've had a passion for reading biographies and hearing true-life stories. Thus, it was natural for my doctoral research to focus on the healing powers of memoir writing and the effects of early significant experiences. Many of the writers whom I interviewed for my research said their life's work was inspired by significant pivotal childhood experiences. For example, poet Kim Stafford, the author of *100 Tricks Every Boy Can Do* (2012), said that since childhood his life theme has been *kuleana*, or, as he describes it, "the freedom to tell stories." *Kuleana* has also been described as a "privilege," a "concern," or a "responsibility" (p. 174).

When writing about his brother's suicide, Stafford realized that the experience of writing and telling his stories gave him a palpable freedom. Also, ever since he was a young boy, he has loved posing questions. He admitted that while writing his memoir, he asked questions to help him make sense of his life and his brother's suicide. Through writing, he also realized the importance of transparency in his life, and he figured out why his father never discussed his brother's death. He suspected it was because of his father's upbringing during the Great Depression. People thought differently in those days, and suicide was considered a taboo subject that was rarely discussed.

~ ~ ~

Sometimes it's good to stop and examine our lives to put us in deeper connection with our consciousness. If you're considering doing so, here are some questions you might ask yourself:

- What did I enjoy doing during my childhood?
- What is my soul's purpose?
- To what do I want to consecrate my life?
- What am I most grateful for?

Throughout my life, I believe I have intuitively asked these questions. As a young teen, I was drawn to spiritual books, movies, and documentaries about consciousness, meditation, and following one's intuition. During my second year of college, I attended a lecture on Transcendental Meditation (TM) inspired by Maharishi Yogi. I'd read about this style of meditation and knew that, of all the various forms of meditation, TM has a solid base of scientific research. Maharishi was a longtime seeker, and his lecture was geared toward kindred spirits like me. I felt comfortable in the room. I had a sense that, for one reason or another, we were all seekers of the absolute and ultimate truth. We also yearned to know life's purpose. We intuitively knew it was connected to happiness—but how were we to find this happiness? I understood that suffering was the opposite of bliss, and I wanted to do everything in my power to bring the latter into my life.

"Pure consciousness is an infinite reservoir of creativity and intelligence and is the ultimate, unified level of being, which is the true self of everything and everyone," said Maharishi. To reach transcendence, he advocated the importance of going deep within yourself during meditation. He said that, ultimately, this is where we experience peace, happiness, and freedom from limitations.

After the lecture, I scheduled an appointment for a private session with a teacher who gave me my personal mantra. She told me not to share it with anybody. For the past four decades, on and off, I've meditated using this mantra. In addition to my connection to nature and birds, my meditation practice has saved me during very turbulent times. Focusing on a mantra or the breath is the most common meditation practice. This prevents us from being distracted by thoughts or mental preoccupations.

Basically, meditation is actively doing nothing, maintaining a sense of stillness, and halting mental activities. One might assume that it is akin to an unconscious state, but the opposite is true. Meditation is the state of being completely awake; thus, consciousness is what meditation is all about. It also allows us to be in touch with our five senses, and we achieve joy through being tuned in. Increasing our sense of consciousness results in the ability to leave negative emotions behind. It's about letting go. You'll know you're more conscious when you aren't thrown off balance by disturbances in your environment but instead remain grounded and levelheaded.

Through meditation, I learned to be not only positive but also calm and nonreactive in stressful situations. I learned how to keep things simple and how to keep an open mind. I also learned the importance of using my heart over my head as a gateway to being conscious.

Maharishi inspired me, just as Viktor Frankl did, to find the purpose and meaning in my life. As a seasoned elder now, I've come to realize we're all brought here for a reason. While some of us know our reason early on, it takes others their entire life to find it. One of my life purposes, like my grandmother's, is nurturing and healing. I also know that, as a writer, my words and stories heal others. In my memoir-writing workshops, I help others ascertain their life purpose by providing writing prompts to inspire reflection.

In his book *One Unbounded Ocean of Consciousness* (2021), Tony Nader, a leader of the Maharishi Foundation, says that without consciousness, "there is no questioning, no choice, no freedom, no responsibility. There would neither be dreams, feelings, hopes, desires, pain nor joy. Consciousness is the indispensable screen that expresses, upholds, and even shapes all knowledge and experience" (p. 8).

He deftly says, "Awareness. Alertness. Attention. Focus. Wakefulness. We can recognize these are all aspects of Consciousness." He adds that, simply put, consciousness is the ability to be aware of something, to be awake, and to be able to evaluate both ourselves and our environment. "Consciousness exists, Consciousness is all there is, and Consciousness is conscious," he concludes (p. 42).

The timely release of his book during the coronavirus pandemic reminded me of the ongoing importance of interconnectedness and the hopeful idea that, as a society, we are becoming more aware, more conscious, and perhaps more compassionate. None of us lives in a vacuum. Was the timing of the pandemic purposeful? It's given us an opportunity to reorganize our priorities, understand what's important, and let go of what no longer serves us. All this takes a heightened state of awareness. As Rebecca Solnit said in her 2020 article, "The Impossible Has Already Happened: What Coronavirus Can Teach Us About Hope," about the pandemic:

> When a storm subsides, the air is washed clean of whatever particulate matter has been obscuring the view, and you can often see farther and more sharply than at any other time. When the storm clears, we may, as do people who have survived a serious illness or accident, see where we were and where we should go in a new light. We may feel

free to pursue change in ways that seemed impossible while the ice of the status quo was locked up. We may have a profoundly different sense of ourselves, our communities, our systems of production and our future.

To be able to have a different sense of ourselves, we must raise our level of consciousness. There are many books and articles on how to do so. Years ago, I learned a practice for it from one of my spiritual guides. The idea is to be in touch with our spiritual or third eye, the point between our eyebrows behind which the frontal lobe of the brain is located. It can be uncomfortable to focus on that spot for a long time, but there's a trick: keep your eyes open and imagine staring at the top of a distant mountain. This method won't strain your eyes but is one way to raise your consciousness when needed. Sometimes I use it if I need to focus on my writing, as it minimizes distractions. It also works well when one is in a state of stillness, such as meditation.

Not only has the pandemic offered us a time to honor stillness, but it's also helped us become reacquainted with ourselves. Prior to the lockdown, most of us were busy with our personal and professional lives and often neglected checking in with our heart center to see what makes us happy. A gift of the pandemic has been to offer us the opportunity to stop and contemplate our lives and what makes our heart sing.

When the vaccine finally made it possible for us to interact more safely with others, I imagine many of us hoped that we'd appreciate the value of direct face-to-face contact more. It's too soon to tell if this has happened. For many, the time of forced aloneness has clarified priorities. It's a common phenomenon that any brush with death brings gratitude. As Rebecca Solnit says in her article noted above, "The proximity of death in shared calamity makes many people more urgently alive, less attached to the small things in life and more committed to the big ones, often including civil society or the common good."

Cancer patients are acutely aware of their mortality. They're also compulsive healers and caregivers. They often tend to put others' needs before their own. It's been called the disease of "nice people." Bernie Siegel says in his book, *Love, Medicine and Miracles* (2011), that one of the most common precursors of cancer is a traumatic loss. Another precursor can also be a feeling of emptiness in one's life. He uses the example of a salamander losing a limb and growing a new one. In a similar way, when a human suffers from an emotional loss that is not dealt with, the body very often responds by developing a new growth, such as cancer.

I've always thought of myself as being not only a highly conscious person but also one who possesses good instincts. Many people ask my opinion on various issues. It's easy for me to tap into my higher self for answers—and, yes, these traits were inherited from my grandmother.

Reflections / Writing Prompts

1. What transformative childhood event has affected you for the rest of your life?

2. In keeping with the premise that we're all brought here for a reason and have a life purpose, what would you say yours is?

3. If tomorrow were your last day on Earth, how would you spend it?

4. What childhood passions have you carried with you into adulthood?

5. What are your feelings and thoughts about conditional and unconditional love?

15   Our Legacies

I am what survives me.

~ Erik Erikson

We all stand on the shoulders of giants. When looking back at my own ancestors, I believe I'm honoring their wisdom by working hard, being compassionate, and listening to the messages of my heart. I have been blessed to have known my maternal grandparents who, as I've described, were survivors of two world wars and who shared their stories and life perspectives with me in journals and during dinner conversations. I want to continue to emulate those who came before me and bestow the gift of perspective and hope. Sometimes, when our ancestors pass away, they become our spirit guides. This is how I reconnected with my father and maternal grandmother. As I journey through the second cancer diagnosis of my life, I wonder how my own grandchildren will connect with me when I'm gone.

At the age of sixty-two, I was blessed with my first grandchild, whose middle name honored my father-in-law who passed away years earlier. Since then, I've been blessed with five more grandchildren. Two of my grandsons have their great-grandfathers' middle names, both of whom were Holocaust survivors. It's such a wonderful feeling when your children name their child after a deceased loved one— which is quite common in the Jewish culture. My biggest fear after being diagnosed with smoldering multiple myeloma in 2006 was that I'd never get to meet my grandchildren, so their arrival has been a bonus blessing. My dream to become a grandparent to carry the torch of previous generations has been manifested.

In my lifetime, I will have seen across five generations, less than some and more than others. Quoting again Mary Pipher in *Women Growing North* (2019), she says she was lucky to have seen across seven generations and that this long view of her family has helped her reflect on questions such as, "What is temperament?" "What are the effects of parenting?" "Of culture?" "What is in the blood?" and "How did I come to be who I am today?" (p. 233). These are questions I have also pondered while writing this book.

I feel honored to have seen my children become wonderful parents. It's never easy becoming a parent, but the added pressure of bringing a child into the world during a pandemic presents a new set of obstacles. Most parents are mindful of disease transmission when their child is an infant, but it's terrifying when there's a deadly virus out there that we know little about. As a quarantine baby, my fifth grandchild didn't have much interaction with anyone outside his immediate family. Before his parents were vaccinated, they met only with masked visitors in the backyard. By the time he turned eight months old, both his parents were vaccinated. Even though visitors were finally allowed into the house, eight-month-olds are typically afraid of strangers. So, this fact—coupled with having had no visitors in the months prior—resulted in him being extra scared of strangers.

During the coronavirus pandemic, I thought a lot about my grandma and wondered how she managed during the cholera pandemic. While she wasn't a young mother, but was left to look after her younger sister after their parents died. She had to grow up quickly. I think of how she and her sister moved from Poland to Vienna to live closer to their older brothers, who rejected them, resulting in their living in an orphanage. I wonder how her ancestors of place affected the person she became.

My grandmother was beautiful and entered modeling school in Vienna, Austria during her adolescence, which is where she met my grandfather, also a model. They married in 1927 when she was twenty-four and he was thirty. In her journal, she said she married for security, not for love. In 1930, my mother was born, and, in 1939, the three of them emigrated to the United States, speaking only a few words of English. Regardless of the century, being an immigrant comes with enormous challenges and obstacles.

Being an empathetic and aware person especially comes in handy when you're a grandmother. You need to be steeped in the present. Children are great teachers of mindfulness practice because they live in the moment. This is what my Los Angeles–based grandchildren taught me when they lived with us for six months during the pandemic. Being with them was grounding. Children have a way of bringing us back to what's important.

Children can also teach us to be in touch with our inner child, affording us a time to pause and ask ourselves what our inner child needs. Maybe our inner child needs to play more, read more, or dream more. I often stop to reflect on what my inner child needs, and I frequently write about it in my journals and urge my students to do the same. In Thich Nhat Hanh's book *Reconciliation* (2010), the late wise Buddhist said that inside each of us is a young, suffering child and that we suffer because we've not been touched by understanding and compassion. To protect ourselves from future suffering, we all try to forget the pain, but sometimes our inner, wounded child calls out to us. When this happens, he suggests going back to our inner child to tell them you are taking care of them.

You can take care of your inner child by writing from your inner child's point of view. This gives a voice to your pain. Sometimes that's all the pain needs. Other times, the inner child might need to be addressed through deeper psychological work. Acknowledging the inner child means treating him or her with respect and love. You can do this by saying, "I love you," "I hear you," "I'm sorry you feel this way," and "Thank you for being you."

~ ~ ~

Since my grandmother's death in the early 1960s, there have been so many sociological and political changes. Despite the chaos and sense of uncertainty in the world right now, I want to provide my grandchildren with a safe haven. Two of the most important gifts we can give and receive are love and comfort. I want to buy them their first journals, as my mother did for me. I want them to have a place of refuge whether they choose to write or draw—an art-filled space that acts as a nonjudgmental confidante. I want to teach them how to do needlepoint, as my grand-mother taught me.

Needlepoint is clearly a creative endeavor, but it's also a meditative practice and a way of clearing my mind, as is going for a walk or gardening. As Sonia Choquette says in her book, *Ask Your Guides* (2006), these types of activities divert our attention from mind chatter and in a sense give us a break. She also claims that these activities will always connect us to our Higher Selves.

From what I know about my grandmother and the messages she's shared, I do believe that her needlepoint practice was her way to cope with the chaos around her. I still have four needlepoint chair cusions that she made nearly one hundred years ago. In keeping with the family tradition, when each of my grandchildren was born, I made them their own needlepoint pillow with an especially chosen design. For my first grandson, I made a Raggedy Andy pillow because, as a kid, I was a big fan of these dolls. For my first granddaughter, I made a pillow featuring Raggedy Anne. Next, I made a colorful elephant, then a zebra, and, most recently, a caterpillar for my third grandson.

While continuing my legacy of Raggedy Anne dolls, which I bought for each of my children when they were young, I also observe other traces of my heritage in my own children. My son is a writer, editor, and publisher. Both his older sisters are entrepreneurs who've merged my creative gene with their father's and grandfather's entrepreneurial gene. As I sit with the dream of passing on my legacy, I cannot help but wonder what professions each of my grandchildren will choose. Will one of them be a writer? What will inspire them to be so and how will the new world of AI affect their chosen profession?

I wrote my first book in 1983 when pregnant with my first daughter. My obstetrician had ordered me to adhere to a regimen of strict bed rest due to a congenital uterine abnormality called "bicornate uterus with an incompetent cervix." Prior to bed rest, I had to go to the hospital to have a suture put into my cervix so that I wouldn't miscarry—as I'd done three years earlier because of this condition I hadn't known I had. After a short stint as the director of nursing in a chronic-care hospital, I'd had to resign.

Having always had a job outside the home, I was now restricted to our bed. Simon, the inventor, built me a slanted desk made of pine to fit over my expanding belly. The desk supported my black Smith Corona typewriter, where I typed that first book. I spent most of my day propped up in bed writing. I kept the completed pages in a large, loose-leaf binder and, years later, when Simon bought me my first computer, I transcribed them all. As strange as this might sound, mine was the first trade book about high-risk pregnancies. All the other books were medical texts, and, in those days before the Internet, women had to rely solely on information provided by their obstetrician.

After numerous attempts to interest large publishers in this self-help book, I decided to self-publish. Those were the days before people knew what that term meant, but I was blessed that Simon was an engineer, and he helped me bring the book to fruition. We produced the book with Ventura Publisher, and it was released in 1986. After the hard copies were printed, I put on my creative-marketing hat and sold more than ten thousand copies from my basement in Montreal. I used what was then called direct-mail advertising, sending out thousands of letters via snail mail to announce my new book. It was a huge amount of work, but getting my book noticed by the media and being interviewed was very rewarding.

Instead of hiring a graphic designer for the cover, I asked my eldest daughter, who was four at the time, to help me. I bought her a new box of watercolor paints and a big piece of unruled art paper and told her to make a cover for Mommy's first book. She looked up at me with her bright, hazel eyes and big smile and said, "Okay."

Now more than thirty-five years later, she's still as methodical as she was then. I handed her the paper and she took it, adjusting it to the perfect angle for painting. Studying the circles of color on the palette, she tried to decide which one to use first. One by one, she tried each color, making sweeping, diagonal, artistic lines across the page, and created an original masterpiece. I received hundreds of compliments on her cover art.

Recently I was reminded of this project when my then four-year-old granddaughter visited. On the kitchen counter near her art closet sat a stack of white KN95 masks. I told her that I'd begun writing a new book and that a hummingbird was the main character. She loves books, so I could see the wheels in her brain turning at a quick pace.

"Sweetheart, I have all these white masks. Would you like to color them to look like hummingbirds for me?"

"Sure," she said, with her radiant, big smile and her brown eyes looking into up into mine.

"DeeDee [what my grandchildren call me], can you lift me on the stool?"

Placing her on the stool near the high counter, I set her up with a new box of crayons, their fragrance eliciting a flood of memories from my own childhood. After coloring the four masks with her usual confidence and enthusiasm, she looked at me for my reaction and said, "Finished."

"Those are so beautiful. Thank you so much!"

She glowed with joy and a sense of accomplishment.

Patience is required when doing art projects with children, but it's worth the time and effort. The joy I glean from creating art with my grandchildren always reminds me that adults need to slow down. The time I spend with them and their parents is precious. Indeed, as I grow older, I realize that time is our most valuable commodity.

My father instinctively understood this truth. Without being asked, he'd get down on the floor and play for hours with my three children when they were small. You can learn a lot when watching children play. While the toys have changed over the years, some hobbies and activities, such as gardening, are ageless. My grandchildren love planting seeds in the garden. My eldest grandson grows herbs on his backyard terrace in Florida, and his mother often asks him to collect some before dinner. He proudly slides open the glass door, grabs a handful, and brings them to the kitchen. He's in awe watching them grow and then finally being able to eat them. Because I'm a continent away, I watch this on FaceTime.

The pandemic brought many challenges regarding my connection with my two Florida-based grandchildren. Not knowing how long the pandemic would last, I didn't know when, how, or if I could see them. Figuring out how to be a long-distance grandparent was difficult and anxiety producing. I gathered ideas from articles and books. I plastered my home with photos of my grandchildren in an effort to permeate my surroundings with their youthful and vibrant energy. To remain connected, we frequently FaceTimed.

While modern technology helped bridge distances during the pandemic, many of us forget to offer gratitude to the techies of the world. Simon often reminds me to do this. Staying true to old-fashioned ways, I often send my grandchildren greetings cards via snail mail, trying to teach them the power of the written word.

We bond differently with different grandchildren in the same way that we bond differently with different people. We might feel more connected to one grandchild than we do another, and that's okay. I've been warned not to play favorites. When people ask which is my favorite grandchild, I say, "My favorite is the one I'm with." This covers all my bases.

As I write this, all my grandchildren are seven and under, but I already sense a special and unique connection with each one. I focus on each child as an individual, trying to understand their unique ways and needs. In the years to come, I look forward to deepening our relationships until the day when I can introduce them to my passion for journaling. I'd love to be around long enough to see them write a first poem or publish a first book. I'm nearly nine years older than my grandmother was when she took her life. I often feel as if time is running out, but my hope is that it's not. I trust that all the latest medical advances will help me thrive until a ripe old age.

I hope that when my grandchildren are older, they'll be curious enough to ask me questions about my life before they were born. Few people take the time to sit down with their grandparents and hold space for them so they can share their stories. I want to teach my grandchildren the art of listening as a way to *really* hear stories. From an early age, my nephew has understood this art. He's interesting *and* interested. He loves stories, which probably explains why he studied film at Columbia University Film School. I've seen him listen to his grandmothers for hours as they share their life stories. It's mutually enjoyable for all involved. Hearing about other people's lives is empowering. Mythologist Joseph Campbell believed that the stories and myths we grow up with become the tracks on which ideals and possibilities are formed.

Many of my stories began on the pages of my journals. My legacy includes six decades of journals that fill big, plastic storage boxes in my writing-studio closet. Some of my most transformative life experiences and stories, such as my losses and cancer journeys, are in my published books. Perhaps, one day, my children and grandchildren will be inspired to read through my journals and books. But then I wonder, what if reading on paper becomes a thing of the past, and they use all my books and journals to start bonfires? But of course not! That is my writer's imagination at work. I want to believe that they'll want to know me through the words I penned to paper.

At this point in my life, I've had much time to reflect on the events of my past and my relationships with loved ones. I spent decades blaming and trying to understand my mother—how and why she fostered my low self-esteem—and feeling angry because she wasn't the picture-perfect mom. I've come to a certain resolve, which began when I buried her spirit with my friend. My mother taught me about my own power and reminded me that if you set your mind to it, you can survive and thrive in almost any situation. I also believe we come into this world with a blueprint that is our guiding light. What's most important is how we react to it, what we do with those experiences, and what we learn from them.

As my mother enters her ninety-forth year, she begins to show signs of dementia. A silver lining to her condition is that she has become more loving and often expresses gratitude rather than anger toward me. While she has never really forgiven me for putting her in an assisted-living facility, I think she realizes that I did it out of love. She actually takes the time to thank me when I call, and this means so much to me. Just yesterday, my husband said he hopes she will stick around a lot longer to make up for all the love she didn't give me in the past.

For that and many other reasons, I've made the conscious decision to forgive my mother for the person she was to me. I realize she did her best with her blueprint. I try to focus on the positives she brought into my life, such as giving me my first journal and sending me when I was fifteen to the International Teen Camp in Switzerland, where I met teens from around the world and watched Neil Armstrong walk on the moon. Most importantly, she sent me to Canada to work, where I met Simon, my soulmate who has changed and shaped my life forever. I don't want my mother to leave this universe thinking that she did me harm. I've thanked her where thanks are due. I've let go of the bad things she did to me, but I share them so that people know from where I have come.

I am grateful for her late-onset sense of gratitude for me. These days, she thanks me for gifts and flowers that I send and for making doctor appointments for her. She no longer takes me for granted. I've been told that those with dementia often have a personality shift and I'm warmed to feel a type of motherly love that I did not feel as a child.

As a sexagenarian with multiple myeloma, I'm unsure how much time I have left in this planet. The literature says that those with this disease don't usually live more than twenty-five years beyond their diagnosis, which means I might have eight years left. Surely, I want to defy all statistics, but I'm living in the moment and lowering my expectations. I do want to make the most of this next chapter of my life.

For many people, the fear of death looms large. When faced with war, illness, or a pandemic, death is often the inevitable outcome. I've never been afraid of death. I'm more afraid of pain.

I believe that living with hope can save us. My ancestors taught me this. We age like we live. We're a combination of our former selves, selves who—like feathers in the breeze—integrate into our souls and give shape and substance to who we are in any given moment. All my lived experiences have helped me to evolve and made me wiser, which I hope graciously to pass on to my grandchildren.

Because of my health challenges, one important message that I want to relay to my grandchildren is the importance of taking care of their bodies, minds, and spirits. My father used to say, "Without your health, you don't have anything at all." I also want to show them the importance of remaining curious and to teach them that no question is a stupid question. As a child, my mother ridiculed me when I asked questions. I want my grandchildren to feel safe to ask me any question that comes to them. I want to teach them the importance of reading, traveling, and gathering different perspectives throughout their lifetimes.

I take the same approach with the college students who work for me. Since moving to California, I've hired college students as personal assistants because they are enthusiastic and quick learners in technology. I live near the University of Southern California, Santa Barbara, and sponsor the Raab Fellows Program, which offers mentoring and research opportunities in writing to selected undergraduates. The students come from many disciplines, and the studies they choose to undertake are fascinating. Most of them want to have careers as writers, editors, or publishers. This gives me access to talented students with interests similar to mine. In turn, they are honored to work alongside a writer. One of them, in fact, inspired the creation of one of my recent projects, *Conversation Cards for Meaningful Storytelling*.

One day, when this student came to work, I asked her how her weekend was. She told me that she had seen her grandmother but was feeling frustrated. "I love visiting my grandmother. Each time I visit, I ask her to tell me stories, but she has trouble sharing."

"What stories do you want to hear?" she said her grandmother asks. "I just have so many."

The student had no idea what questions to ask. We thought that if she had this problem, certainly others did, too. We brainstormed about how to help her and came up with conversation-starter cards. We created a series of questions and had them professionally printed on four-by-four cards with a different prompt/question on each one coupled with beautiful feather (my icon) illustrations. The decks are housed in decorative boxes now available on Amazon and other websites. The student said that on her next visit with her grandmother, she took a deck, and they were truly helpful in inspiring her grandmother's stories. They were both extremely grateful.

I want to teach my grandchildren the importance of nurturing happiness and how being grateful contributes to happiness. I want to pass on all my values—of being a good person, of being honest, of nurturing yourself and your family. Most importantly, I want to teach my grandchildren to savor every moment of their lives, to live fiercely and with a sense of purpose. It is difficult to explain to young children that their journey will be over before they know it, but we can teach by example; we can insist, via our own behavior, that they live a life abundant.

As I arrive at the last chapter of this book, we've all realized that the pandemic is behind us, but that the virus will be around for many years to come. Some people wear masks and others do not. It has become a personal choice. It's no longer mandated on airplanes, although I feel most safe with my mask on. We have all learned a lot during the past few years. Many have taken the time to figure out what's important to them, what to work on, and what they want to let go of. Some are tapping into and exploring new passions. Many people have devoted more time to self-care. Most of us have adapted to a new way of being.

Through the experience, we've hopefully gained an added respect and sense of interconnectedness with one another. It seems like a good time to reflect on what we learned from the experience and how our life perspectives have changed. I've always believed that it's not so much what happens to you but how you react to your experiences that matters.

My hope is that my grandchildren all flourish and that their lives are always surrounded by love. I hope that after I leave this physical plane, I, like my grandmother, will visit my grandchildren, perhaps as a hummingbird, perhaps as a dragonfly, or perhaps only in these written recollections, visitations, and collected wisdoms. My wish is also that the story of my grandmother and me provides hope and perspective for readers and future generations.

I look out my writing studio's window. My visiting hummingbird is flitting through the red blossoms, but, momentarily, to my astonishment, it flips upside down, its colors a rainbow of memories. My grandmother is telling me it's time to end this story but that others will surely follow, and that goodbyes, if we open our hearts to the possibility, are only temporary.

Reflections / Writing Prompts

1. Write about some of your ancestors of family, spirit, and place.

2. If you were to live your life over again, how might you live it differently?

3. Share the stories of how your parents and grandparents met.

4. In what ways are you in touch with your inner child?

5. What important life lessons do you want to pass on to future generations?

About the Author

Diana Raab, MFA, PhD, is a memoirist, poet, blogger, speaker, and award-winning author of thirteen books. Her work has been widely published and anthologized. She frequently speaks and writes about writing for healing and transformation. Many of her talks are based on her book, *Writing for Bliss: A Seven-Step Plan for Telling Your Story and Transforming Your Life,* and its accompanying book, *Writing for Bliss: A Companion Journal.*

Raab, who has been writing for nearly six decades, blogs *for Psychology Today, The Wisdom Daily, The Good Men Project,* and *Thrive Global.* She is a guest blogger on many other sites. She's the author of two memoirs—*Regina's Closet: Finding My Grandmother's Secret Journal* and *Healing with Words: A Writer's Cancer Journey* as well as five poetry collections, including *An Imaginary Affair: Poems Whispered to Neruda.* She's also the editor of two anthologies: *Writers and Their Notebooks* and *Writers on the Edge.* Visit https://dianaraab.com.

References

Addonizio, K. (2009). *Ordinary genius: A guide for the poet within.* New York, NY: W. W. Norton.

Aurobindo, S. (1990). *The mother.* Twin Lakes, WI: Lotus Press.

Choquette, S. (1999). *The wise child: A spiritual guide to nurturing your child's intuition.* New York: Three Rivers Press.

Choquette, S. (2006). *Ask your guides.* Carlsbad, CA: Hay House, Inc.

Epstein, H. (1988). *Children of the holocaust: Conversations with sons and daughters of survivors.* New York, NY: Penguin Books.

Epstein, M. (1995). *Thoughts without a thinker: Psychotherapy from a Buddhist perspective.* New York, NY: Basic Books.

Foor, D. (2017). *Ancestral medicine: Rituals for personal and family healing.* Rochester, VT: Bear & Co.

Frankl, V. E. (2006). *Man's search for meaning.* Boston: Beacon Press.

Gregor, M. (with Stone, G.). (2015). *How not to die: Discover the foods scientifically proven to prevent and reverse disease.* New York, NY: Flatiron Books.

Hanh, T. N. (2010). *Reconciliation: Healing the inner child.* Berkeley, CA: Parallax Press.

Nader, T. (2021). *One unbounded ocean of consciousness: Simple answers to the big questions in life.* New York, NY: Penguin Books.

Nin, A. (1976). *The diary of Anaïs Nin, volume five, 1947–1955.* New York, NY: Houghton Mifflin Harcourt.

Pipher, M. (2019). *Women rowing north: Navigating life's currents and flourishing as we age.* New York, NY: Bloomsbury.

Raab, D. (2020). How illness can be lonely and what to do about it. *Tiny Buddha.* tinybuddha.com/blog/how-illness-can-be-lonely-what-to-do-about-it/.

Rilke, R. M. (1993). *Letters to a young poet.* (M. D. Herter Norton, Trans.). New York, NY: W. W. Norton.

Siegel, B. (2011). *Love, medicine and miracles: Lessons learned about self-healing from a surgeon's experience with exceptional patients.* New York, NY: HarperCollins.

Solnit, R. (2020, April 7). The impossible has already happened: What coronavirus can teach us about hope. *The Guardian.* www.theguardian.com/world/2020/apr/07/what-coronavirus-can-teach-us-about-hope-rebecca-solnit.

Tippett, K. (Host). (2017, November 9). Rachel Yehuda: How trauma and resilience cross generations. *On Being.* https://onbeing.org/programs/rachel-yehuda-how-trauma-and-resilience-cross-generations-nov2017/.

Stafford, K. (2012). *100 tricks every boy can do: A memoir.* San Antonio, TX: Trinity University Press.

Van der Kolk, B. (2014). *The body keeps score: Brain, mind, and body in the healing of trauma.* New York, NY: Penguin Books.

Writing for Bliss is most funda-
mentally about reflection, truth,
and freedom. With techniques and
prompts for both the seasoned and
novice writer, it will lead you to

- tap into your creativity
  through storytelling and
  poetry,

- examine how life-
  changing experiences can
  inspire writing,

- pursue self-examination
  and self-discovery through the written word, and,

- understand how published writers have been
  transformed by writing.

"Part writing guide, part memoir, and part love letter to
the craft of writing, Diana Raab's *Writing for Bliss* is a
caring and motivational guide. Raab's love of words and
her belief in the power of story shine through. With its
hypnotic and personal stories, interviews with other
authors, and many useful writing prompts, *Writing for
Bliss* will find a valued spot on the bookshelves of those
seeking greater understanding."
—ANGELA WOLTMAN, *Foreword Reviews*

"By listening to ourselves and being aware of what we
are saying and feeling, the true story of our life's past
experience is revealed. Diana Raab's book gives us the
insights by which we can achieve this through her life-
coaching wisdom and our writing."
—BERNIE SIEGEL, MD, author of *The Art of Healing*

From Loving Healing Press
Paperback * hardcover * eBook * audiobook

DIANA M. RAAB and JAMES BROWN, editors

Writers on the Edge offers a range of essays, memoirs and poetry written by major contemporary authors who bring fresh insight into the dark world of addiction, from drugs and alcohol, to sex, gambling and food. Editors Diana M. Raab and James Brown have assembled an array of talented and courageous writers who share their stories with heartbreaking honesty as they share their obsessions as well as the awe-inspiring power of hope and redemption.

"Open to any piece in this collection, and the scalding, unflinching, overwhelming truths within will shine light on places most people never look. Anyone who reads this book, be they users or used, will put it down changed. And when they raise their eyes from the very last page, the world they see may be redeemed, as well."
—JERRY STAHL, author of *Permanent Midnight*

"*Writers on the Edge* is a thoughtful compendium of first-person narratives by writers who have managed to use their despair to create beauty. A must-read for anyone in the recovery field."
—LEONARD BUSCHEL, Founder, Writers in Treatment

CONTRIBUTORS: Frederick and Steven Barthelme, Kera Bolonik, Margaret Bullitt-Jonas, Maud Casey, Anna David, Denise Duhamel, B. H. Fairchild, Ruth Fowler, David Huddle Perie Longo, Gregory Orr, Victoria Patterson, Molly Peacock, Scott Russell Sanders, Stephen Jay Schwartz, Linda Gray Sexton, Sue William Silverman, Chase Twichell, and Rachel Yoder

From Modern History Press

Healing With Words: A Writer's Cancer Journey is a compassionate and wry self-help memoir written by an award-winning prolific author, nurse and poet, who at the age of forty-seven found her life shattered first by a DCIS (early breast cancer) diagnosis and five years later by another, seemingly unrelated and incurable cancer—multiple myeloma. The book includes the author's experiences, reflections, poetry and journal entries, in addition to writing prompts for readers to express their own personal story. Raab's journals have provided a safe haven and platform to validate and express her feelings. Raab views journaling to be like a daily vitamin—in that it heals, detoxifies and is essential for optimal health.

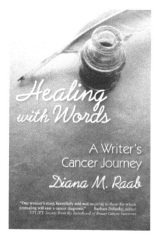

Readers will learn to:

- understand the importance of early cancer detection and how to take control of their own health,

- discover the power of writing to release bottled-up emotions,

- learn how the process of journaling can facilitate healing,

- see how a cancer diagnosis can be a riveting event which can renew and change a person in a unique way.

"One woman's story, beautifully told and inspiring to those for whom journaling will ease a cancer diagnosis."
—BARBARA DELINSKY, author *UPLIFT: Secrets from the Sisterhood of Breast Cancer Survivors*

Printed in the USA
CPSIA information can be obtained
at www.ICGtesting.com
JSHW012112291223
54521JS00005B/12

9 781615 997640